Life

Topics

ックス5

Nathan Berman

Changing Views

NAN'UN-DO

Life Topics: Changing Views
総合英語　ライフ トピックス 5

*This book is dedicated to you, the students,
without whose help it would not have been possible.*

このテキストの音声を無料で視聴（ストリーミング）・ダウンロード
できます。自習用音声としてご活用ください。
以下のサイトにアクセスしてテキスト番号で検索してください。

https://nanun-do.com　テキスト番号 [**512170**]

※ 無線 LAN（WiFi）に接続してのご利用を推奨いたします。

※ 音声ダウンロードは Zip ファイルでの提供になります。
お使いの機器によっては別途ソフトウェア（アプリケーション）
の導入が必要となります。

※ Life Topics: Changing Views 音声ダウンロードページは以下の
QR コードからもご利用になれます。

Read by

Ryan Drees

LIFE TOPICS
CHANGING VIEWS

* Flexible, innovative exercises strengthen essential language skills while developing social skills and boosting self-confidence through honest, cordial discussions and debate.

* Enlightening, absorbing topics—forming good habits, building friendships, increasing personal productivity, managing stress, and many others— encourage learners to examine their own lives and characters and to respect those of others, fostering a more inclusive, more compassionate world view.

* Clear, concise, accessible English and workbook-like layouts and outlines allow teachers to custom-make each unit's many interactive, guided-composition activities for all language-ability levels.

© Jonathan Berman

"The unexamined life is not worth living."
– Socrates

CONTENTS
目次

1

The Joys of Anticipation
期待の喜び

◆ Pre-Reading Questions

1. Does it make you happy to anticipate something positive that may happen to you in the future?

2. Which makes you happier: thinking about something that happened to you in the past, or thinking about something similar that may happen to you in the future? For example, which makes you happier: remembering last year's birthday celebration, or anticipating next year's birthday celebration? Explain why.

◆ Vocabulary

1. Anticipating 期待する   2. Imagine 想像する   3. Nostalgia 懐かしさ
4. Pleasure 喜び   5. Source of happiness 幸せの源

◆ **Fill in each blank in the paragraph below with the correct word or phrase. Make sure you use the appropriate word forms.**

Jan and Jim are now **(a)** _____ traveling to some far away distant island. Two years ago, they went to Okinawa, and they remember that trip with **(b)** _____. They had great **(c)** _____ while swimming in the ocean and playing in the sand. Next year they are **(d)** _____ going to Bali, and that it will give them a great **(e)** _____.

◆ Reading 🎧 02

[1] **Anticipation** is an important **source of happiness**. It increases our enjoyment of any event, whether large or small. **Anticipation** is the joy you feel while looking forward to a future event. You should try to enjoy this added happiness for as long as you can, because when you do so, you are, in a way, experiencing the **pleasure** of an event before it actually happens.

[2] For example, if you were to buy a chocolate bar and then eat it right away, you would, of course, get **pleasure** from the act of eating it. But if you were to wait a few hours to eat it, you would get **pleasure** from both eating the chocolate and from your **anticipation** of eating it, giving you an extra, "free" **source of happiness**.

[3] When you are planning a trip, you may **imagine** all of the different things that could happen. The more you plan, the happier you become. According to certain studies, people who spend more time planning the details of a trip are generally happier than those who don't. It was also found that those who spend time **anticipating** future positive events are, by and large, happier.

[4] **Imagine** that you have decided to travel to a small tropical island with some friends. You may plan where to stay, shop, sightsee, and dine out, or which beaches to visit, what special events to attend, and what to do if the weather is bad. You could happily end up planning this trip for months ahead of time. Such careful "research" often gives us greater **pleasure** than just suddenly going somewhere with no planning. Once you arrive at your destination, you can then compare what you expected to what you actually find there. It could happen that,  after the **pleasure** of **anticipating** and planning your trip in detail, the actual trip may turn out not as good for all kinds of reasons. The island itself may be crowded. There may be too much traffic. Prices may be too high. And there may even be bugs, snakes, and hungry sharks waiting to "eat you alive."

[5] Thinking about pleasant past events is, of course, also a **source of happiness**. You can,  with feelings of **nostalgia**, remember the last time you met your friends for coffee somewhere, or the time you went skiing in Aizu-Wakamatsu. We know what happened in the past. We know what an experience was like at the time it happened. By **anticipating** similar events that may happen in the future, we can increase our joy and enhance our experience, giving us even greater happiness. In other words, while we can think back on the past, we are free to **imagine** the future in great creative detail. Happiness is created by **imagining** what might happen and not knowing exactly

what the places, conversations, foods, scenery, and so on that we will experience will be like – and how we will feel when we experience them.

"There is no terror in a bang, only in the anticipation of it." **–Alfred Hitchcock**

◆ Active Outline

1. Anticipation brings you _____ while you are waiting for some event to happen.
   (happiness / sadness)

2. Before getting a new jacket, say to increase your happiness, you _____ wait for as long as possible before actually going out and buying it. **(should / should not)**

3. The longer you anticipate an upcoming event, the _____ you become.
   (happier / sadder / more stressed)

4. You will feel happier if you _____ what to do on a trip. **(plan / do not plan)**

   a. But it often happens that the actual trip ends up being _____ than you expected.
      (better / worse)

5. Thinking about pleasant past events is _____ a source of happiness. **(also / never)**

   a. While we can only _____ the past with nostalgia, we are free to _____ what might happen in the future. **(imagine, remember / remember, imagine)**

◆ Comprehension

1. The more you plan for a future event, the _____ enjoyable it will be.
   (more / less)

2. If you decide to go around Tokyo taking photographs, the more you anticipate the different kinds of pictures you will take, the _____ you will be. **(sadder / happier)**

3. Between remembering the last movie you saw and thinking about the next movie you will see, it is usually _____ that will make you happier. **(nostalgia / anticipation)**

◆ Discussion / Writing

List three positive future events that you might plan for. (They can be something as simple as going out for dessert with some friends or something as exciting as climbing Mt. Fuji.)

1. _____ 2. _____ 3. _____

I. Choose one of the three future events that you listed above that might happen sometime soon. Then make a plan for it. *Think ahead! Be creative! Use your imagination!*

What I am looking forward to in the future is _____.

What will happen is that I will go to _____. While there, I will

visit _____.

It is my hope (that / to) _____

_____.

II. Describe a past event that you really enjoyed.

The event happened about _____ (days / weeks / months / years) ago. I

went with (my friends / my parents / alone / _____)

(to a park / for coffee / to the beach / on a picnic / to have a meal /

_____). The event took place in the city of _____.

What we ate was _____, and we drank _____

_____. The weather was _____.

It was an (indoor / outdoor) event, and I thought that it was (better / worse) than

I had expected because _____.

The people (with me / whom I noticed around me) were_____

_____. The place smelled like _____

_____. The sounds I heard were _____

_____. What was so (much fun / special / terrible) about the

time was that _____

_____. What I most remember

about that time was that _____

_____.

III. Now anticipate a similar event that might happen in the future. (Plan ahead and use your imagination.)

The next time that I will do this again will be in _____ (days /

weeks / months / _____). What I look forward to the most is

_____

What I will do to have a better time this time is to _____.

I hope that _____

does not happen the next time. In case it does happen, I will prevent it by

_____.

I hope that this will result in _____.

> **Opinion:** While you were writing the essays above, which did you enjoy more, thinking about the past or anticipating the future? Explain.

"We have to put that time in. You can't snap your fingers and make a friend."
– Jeffrey Hall, University of Kansas

[1] In the first study of its kind, a professor from the University of Kansas wanted to find out how long it takes to make a friend. Making a friend might appear to be a quite simple thing to do. All you have to do is to go out and meet many different people, find someone you like, spend time together, and create a bond! But just how long does it take to do that? And what is the best way to put that time to use? Those are some of the important questions the professor wanted answers to. He found that it takes from 40 to 60 hours to make a **casual friend**, 80 to 100 hours to make a regular friend, and 200 hours or longer to make a close friend. In other words, it takes a good deal of time to develop a close friendship. Of course, there is **no guarantee** that if we spend a lot of time with someone that our relationship will move from one of being just **casual friends** to one of being close friends.

[2] People are naturally social and want to **bond** with one another. The professor found that people who had friends were happier, healthier, and even live longer than those who didn't. For high school or college students, it's most important to have lots of friends of all types, some of whom will become close. As for older people, it is the quality of their friendships, not the number, that is more important.

[3] The hours spent together with classmates or people at work do not appear to count so much in the making of a friendship. Even after spending hundreds of hours together at school or in the office, such relationships may not develop into real friendships. For that to happen, the key is to spend time together outside of class or work, doing different activities together. The professor also found that while talking with others helps create casual **bonds**. However, what really strengthens a relationship are the types of things that we talk about. Gossiping, engaging in **small talk**, and discussing boring topics do not lead to close friendships. Only by discussing **meaningful issues** does a friendship grow stronger. In other words, it is not just the amount of time we spend together that matters. What counts is the quality of that time.

[4] So, how do we go about making "good friends"? One step is to go out more often and to meet other people with similar interests. Then, when you meet someone you like, you should go to different places and have different experiences together. You have to make your new friend a **priority**, because if you do not "meet up" regularly, the close friendship will not happen. And while you may already be very busy and have a lot to do, take the time to find and make a close friend or two. Why? Because as the professor found out, having close friends really matters.

*"Maintaining close relationships is the most important work we do in our lives. Most people on their deathbeds agree." – **Jeffrey Hall***

◆ Active Outline

1. The professor wanted to find out how _____.
   (long it takes to make a friend / many friends a person can have)
   a. He also wanted to discover the best way to spend our _____ with that person.
      (money / energy / time)

2. While we are in school, it is more important for us to have _____ friends.
   (older / close / many / few)

3. Spending time together at work _____ always the best way to become good friends.
   (is / is not)
   a. Spending time with another person doing meaningful things _____ matters in the forming of close bonds. **(really / hardly)**

4. To create a close bond, it is better to have _____ different experiences together.
   (a few / many)

◆ Comprehension

Read the statements below and decide if they are true or false.

1. If you spend a lot of time with someone, a close friendship will automatically develop. **True / False**

2. It takes the same amount of time to make a casual friend, a regular friend, or a close friend. **True / False**

3. For older people, the most important thing is to have as many friends as possible. **True / False**

4. The type of conversation we have with others affects the closeness of our friendships with them. **True / False**

5. If we want to become close friends with someone, we need to make developing our friendship with that person a top priority. **True / False**

◆ Critical / Creative Thinking

What parts of the reading do you agree with, disagree with, or have doubts about?

Agree	Disagree / Doubt
1. _____	1. _____
2. _____	2. _____
3. _____	3. _____

> **Opinion: Overall, do you agree or disagree with the ideas expressed in today's reading? Why?**

Overall I (**agree / disagree**) with the ideas. This is because _____

_____ .

◆ Word Scramble

Unscramble the words to make complete sentences.

1. for younger / of friendship / more important / What types / and for older people? / are

   _____

2. meaningful issues, / spend / not / important to / just gossiping. / It is / time discussing

   _____

3. a friend. / long it / to find out how / takes to make / The professor wanted

   _____

4. and mountain climbing / good friend, / do things like / going skiing / you should / To make a / together.

   _____

5. to find and / some ways / friends, and why / What are / make / to do so? / is it important

   _____

◆ Sentence Matching

Match the unscrambled sentences above with the paragraphs in today's reading in which the sentence's information can be found. Note that one sentence is not used.

Paragraph 1. Sentence: _____   Paragraph 2. Sentence: _____

Paragraph 3. Sentence: _____   Paragraph 4. Sentence: _____

◆ Matching

Based on today's reading, match the sentence beginnings and endings.

1. A professor from Kansas wanted to measure ( )
2. He also wanted to know the best way to spend ( )
3. To make a close friend, it takes ( )
4. For college students, it is more important to ( )
5. You can strengthen your friendship ( )
6. You should go out and meet others with ( )
7. You need to see your new friend regularly, or ( )
8. The time spent at work or with classmates does ( )

a. … have many friends.
b. … the friendship may not happen.
c. … how long it takes to make a friend.
d. … by discussing meaningful issues.
e. … our time with a potential friend.
f. … interests similar to yours.
g. … not count much in making close friends.
h. … 200 hours or longer.

◆ Writing Questions

List four interesting conversation topics for you to discuss with a new friend. (*Ex: Is music important to you? Why or why not? Do you take an interest in politics? Why or why not?*)

1. _____ 2. _____

3. _____ 4. _____

◆ Conversation

Now discuss one or two of your topics with a partner or in your group. Write down your partner's answers. Do you agree with their opinions? Explain.

*On the topic of _____ I (**do / do not**) agree with*

their opinions. This is because _____

_____.

*On the topic of _____ I (**do / do not**) agree with*

their opinions. This is because _____

_____.

◆ Discussion / Writing

I. The article states that to make a friend, we should go to different places and have many different experiences with a person. Plan an activity for someone you would like to become good friends with. Where would you go? What would you do? Think of at least three different places you might go to. Be creative and have fun!

When meeting a friend, we would go to _____.

What we would do while there is _____

_____. After that we would go to _____

_____

_____. And finally, we would go to _____

_____. The different experiences and discussions that

we will have during these times together include _____

_____.

II. What are some other ways that we can strengthen our bonds with our friends?

_____

_____

_____

III. What is your best advice for how to make a good friend?

_____

_____

_____

Make up some questions of your own that are related to today's reading. *Be creative!!*

How to Form Good Habits
習慣を作る方法

◆ **Pre-Reading Questions**

Part I : What is the best way to form good habits such as getting more exercise or eating healthier? Explain.

Part II : Are you good at sticking with a good habit you have formed? Explain.

Part III: Do people who can stick to good habits (1) see many temptations around them but have the will power to resist them, or (2) do they arrange their environment so as not to notice the temptations?

◆ **Vocabulary**

1. Behavior 行動　　　2. Repeated 繰り返される　　3. Resist 抵抗

4. Rewards 報酬, 褒美　　5. Willpower 意志力, 自制力

◆ Fill in each blank in the sentences below with the correct word. Make sure you use the appropriate word forms.

a. It was well done and she was given a _____.

b. I have the _____ to stop eating sweets.

c. I must change my _____ and exercise more.

d. We should _____ eating out too often.

e. The teacher _____ the question three times.

◆ Reading 🎧 04

*"Failing to prepare is preparing to fail." — **Benjamin Franklin***

[1] We all have behaviors that we want to replace with good habits, but most of us have no idea how good habits are formed. Perhaps we wish to form some desirable habit. At first it is difficult to do, because we are constantly having to think about it. Later, after we practice the habit, we do it automatically without thinking about it. Such habits can be daily tasks like taking a shower, brushing our teeth, preparing meals, getting dressed, going to work or school, and so on. If we had to re-learn how to do all these things every day, we would be exhausted. While there is a lot of information about habits, most of it is not based on science. Professor Wendy Wood of Southern California has studied habits for over thirty years. Her research has showed her that over 43 percent of the things we do every day are habits. This made her wonder how habits are formed and why so many of us have such a hard time creating and sticking to good habits over the long term. Professor Wood has found that good habits are formed based on three factors: (1) The Environment, (2) Repetition, and (3) Rewards.

[2] **The Environment:** The biggest challenge when we first try to form a new habit is to arrange our environment so we can do the new thing more easily. This includes taking some time to plan ahead so that we can organize our everyday environment in great detail, thereby making the new habit as simple to stick to as possible.

[3] **Repetition:** The more often the habit is repeated, the stronger it becomes. Many goals like becoming healthier, saving money, getting good grades, and so on involve behaviors that must be done often – if possible every day, at the same time of day, and in the same location. Simple habits are picked up faster than more difficult ones. Even the easiest habit (such as eating fruit for dessert instead of cake) can take perhaps two or three months. Something more difficult – like going regularly to the gym – may take six months or even longer.

[4] **Rewards:** While trying to form a new habit, reward yourself by doing something that you enjoy or that you can be proud of. The more rewards you give yourself, the more likely you are to continue. The rewards should be fun and experienced often. This could be something as basic as taking the time to read a novel, enjoying a snack, or while playing chess considering good chess moves. Without rewards, you are unlikely to form the desired habit, even if it is one that could be life-changing.

[5] Most people believe the best way to create good habits is to rely on willpower. Although willpower is important in the beginning, after a certain time we grow tired of maintaining a high level of willpower. Eventually, we lose our willpower altogether.

Unfortunately, when this happens, we often consider ourselves to be weak and a failure. Instead of using **willpower** to **resist** playing a video game, say, or eating some chocolate cookies, the key is to not buy such things in the first place or, if you already have them, to just throw them away. Planning ahead is more important than **willpower**. This means correctly organizing your environment, **repeating** the desired **behaviors** often, and giving yourself **rewards** for small steps toward success. Eventually, the habit will develop to the point where you won't even have to think about it.

"Motivation is what gets you started. Habit is what keeps you going." **– Jim Rohn**

◆ Active Outline

1. At first, desirable new habits are _____ difficult to form. **(more / less)**

    a. While there is a lot of information about how to form habits, most of it _____ based on science. **(is / is not)**

2. It _____ important to plan and organize your surroundings ahead of time. **(is / is not)**

3. The _____ times a behavior is performed, the stronger it becomes. **(more / fewer)**

    a. Picking up a habit that is more difficult to form can take _____ months or longer. **(two / three / six / ten)**

4. We are more likely to stick to habits that are _____. **(important / life-changing / fun)**

    a. If you want to go to the gym regularly but do not like exercise, you _____ likely to continue. **(are / are not)**

5. Having a strong willpower is most important when forming a new habit. **(True / False)**

    a. People who cannot form habits have poor willpower and are failures. **(True / False)**

◆ Critical Thinking

Most daily habits are done without thinking about them. List six of your everyday habits. *(For example, tying my shoelaces, saying good morning, walking to the store.)*

1. _____   2. _____

3. _____   4. _____

5. _____   6. _____

◆ Comprehension

Circle the correct word or phrase in the two paragraphs below.

[1] Most people are **1. (aware / not aware)** of how habits are formed. They believe that **2. (simplifying the environment / willpower)** is needed to create a new good habit. But this **3. (is / is not)** how the mind works. Willpower is overall **4. (very / not very)** important when forming useful habits. Behaviors like **5. (simplifying the environment / exercising willpower)** makes the habit easier to form. To make habits easier to stick to, they **6. (must / must not)** be repeated many times and then **7. (be / not be)** rewarded.

[2] Another strategy is to *Change Your Thinking*. Instead of focusing on having the willpower to resist **8. (sweets / fruits and vegetables)**, you can train yourself to not mentally see them. You tell yourself that such things **9. (are / are not)** for you but are for someone else. Just touching them is **10. (like stealing / a really good idea)**. In other words, if you do not "see" the sweets, for example, you **11. (are / are not)** tempted by them, because to you, they do not even exist. The key is **12. (to / not to)** use willpower but to just ignore them.

◆ **Choose the correct word to form good habits: Environment (E). Repetition (REP). Rewards (REW). Change Your Thinking (C)**

1. Should be done every day. _____
2. There are no sweets in your home. _____
3. There is cake, but you see it as your brother's. _____
4. You move closer to a gym. _____
5. You sleep in running clothes for morning exercise. _____
6. Take pride in cooking. _____
7. Your supermarket is near your yoga class. _____
8. Win at tennis. _____
9. Do a habit the same time every day. _____
10. The habit becomes automatic. _____
11. You walk by the chocolates but do not "see" them. _____
12. You buy fruits are already sliced. _____

◆ **Create some examples of your own.**

_____	_E_
_____	_REP_
_____	_REW_
_____	_C_

◆ Discussion / Comprehension

1. How can you better control your environment? Give examples of what you can do to form good habits and avoid bad habits.

To make forming a good habit like <u>eating fruit</u> more easily, you can <u>get fruit that</u> <u>is pre-cut in the supermarket</u>.

To make forming a good habit like _____ more easily, you can _____

_____.

To make forming a good habit like _____ more easily, you can _____

_____.

To stop a bad habit like <u>having chocolate</u>, do <u>not purchase chocolate or even go</u> <u>into the candy section of a supermarket</u>.

To stop a bad habit like _____, do _____

_____.

2. One study asked: Do people who stick to habits see lots of temptations around but have the willpower to resist them? Or have those people arranged their lives so they do not even notice the temptations?

I believe that the study found that those who stick to habits for a long time will

(**resist / set up their lives to not notice**) all the different temptations around them.

This is because today's article states _____

_____.

◆ Discussion / Writing

I. What habits would you like to form? Make a plan to do so.

_____

_____

_____

II. How successful have you been in forming a new habit?

_____

_____

_____

III. How can you improve your environment to make a new habit easier to form?

_____

_____

_____

Make up some questions of your own that are related to today's reading. Be creative!!

4

How to Become More Productive
生産性を高める方法

◆ **Pre-Reading Question**

When you have a lot of work to do, what is the best way to complete all your task(s)?

◆ **Vocabulary**

1. Daydreaming 空想
2. Distracted 気が散る
3. Efficient 効率的
4. Estimate 見積もり
5. Focus 集中
6. Overwhelming 圧倒的

♦ **Match the sentence beginnings with their endings.**

1. To do a job well, it is important _____
2. Every day Bill sat and stared out the window, _____
3. Whenever the music came on, the students _____
4. The students learned to work hard and became _____
5. Before beginning our job, we had to _____
6. There was so much work to do that _____

a. more **efficient** at getting things done.
b. to **focus** on the work at hand.
c. at times it felt **overwhelming**.
d. became **distracted** and could not think.
e. **daydreaming** of becoming successful.
f. **estimate** how long it takes to complete.

[1] We all want to become more efficient at our jobs and at getting more done, but often we simply do not know how to do it. Perhaps one reason is that we cannot find the proper motivation or focus. Large projects, especially when we first start them, can seem to be overwhelming. One method that appeared in the late 1980s aimed to help people overcome this fear and to become more efficient. Perhaps you've heard of it. It's called The Pomodoro Technique.

[2] Pomodoro is the Italian word for "tomato." The person who came up with this technique used a kitchen timer that was shaped like a tomato. That's where the method's name comes from. Pomodoro is a simple yet powerful technique that is especially effective for doing general-thinking types of assignments such as those we have to do at the high school or university level. The method involves a cycle of work, focus, and then rest. The first step is to break things down into smaller tasks that can be easily done and to then choose one task to do first. To do this, you need a real timer. Set the timer for 25 minutes and then get to work on the task. This session of working time is called a "Pomodoro." During this time, the trick is to focus only on the one single task and not to allow yourself to get distracted. If you do become distracted – if some unrelated ideas pop into your head – write the ideas down on a separate piece of paper and, so you don't think about them, move the paper aside until your Pomodoro session ends.

[3] After finishing each Pomodoro session, you should record it, using, for example, a check mark. Then take a short break of about five minutes. Get up out of your chair and allow yourself to be distracted by having a snack, daydreaming, stretching, or doing something from your "distractions" list. You need these breaks because they allow you to work faster and more efficiently. Without them, your work will become worse. Four Pomodoros make up a "set." After completing a set, take a longer break of 20 to 30 minutes. Perhaps have lunch, or move away from your desk, or just sit doing nothing at all. Then you can begin the process over again as needed, doing the rest of your tasks one at a time.

[4] Before you start a task, you should estimate how many Pomodoros you will need to finish it. There are different ways to do this. You can estimate, for example, that it will take seven Pomodoros to write a paper, including the time you will need to go over and revise what

you have done. Or you can plan to do three Pomodoros in the morning, say, then two in the afternoon, and then four more in the evening. Also, instead of working for only 25 minutes, you can work for 60 or 90 minutes, or any length of time you like, taking shorter or longer breaks as your goals change. Even people who usually work for four or five hours straight will benefit from and become more **efficient** by taking regular breaks after 25 minutes of work. The reason for this is obvious: Taking breaks allows us to concentrate on a single task, thereby improving our **focus** and the outcome of the task itself.

"A Journey of a Thousand Miles Begins with a Single Step." – **Lao Tzu**

◆ Active Outline:

1. Many people have a difficult time completing all the _____ they have to do.
   (fun / work)

2. Pomodoro is an Italian word meaning _____.
   (efficient / motivation / task / tomato)

   a. The inventor of this technique used a tomato-shaped _____.
      (computer / pen / timer)

   b. You should break your _____ tasks down into _____ ones.
      (small, larger / large, smaller)

   c. The period of time called a Pomodoro is when you actually _____.
      (work and focus / become distracted / eat a tomato)

3. After you complete a Pomodoro, you can record it using a _____.
   (check mark / computer)

   a. A Pomodoro "set" consists of _____ Pomodoros. **(one / two / three / four / six)**

   b. You should take a _____ break once you have completed a set. **(longer / shorter)**

4. The reason for taking breaks is they boost your _____.
   (enjoyment / focus / intelligence)

◆ Comprehension

1. The time spent working on and completing a task is called a _____.
   (tomato / distraction / Pomodoro)

2. While in a Pomodoro session you must focus on _____ task(s) at a time.
   (one / two / three / five)

3. Before you begin a task, you _____ estimate how many Pomodoros you will need. **(should / should not)**

4. After each Pomodoro, you should take about a _____ minute break.
   (five / 20 to 30 / 60)

5. After each set you should take a _____ minute break. **(five / 20 to 30 / 60)**

◆ Word Scramble

Unscramble the words to make complete sentences. After you finish, decide if each sentence is True or False.

1. takes a lot / The Pomodoro is / of time / to learn. / technique that / a difficult

   _____ True / False

2. can / 25 minutes to / A Pomodoro / 90 minutes / last from / or longer.

   _____ True / False

3. Pomodoro. / breaks between / take / You must / each

   _____ True / False

4. a Pomodoro, it / email or to make / check your / phone calls. / is OK to / While doing

   _____ True / False

◆ Sequencing

Based on today's reading, put the items below in the proper order. Write the order numbers on the lines, as in the examples.

	Events 1 to 5		Events 6 to 10
___	Work for around a 25-minute Pomodoro session.	___	Complete a "set," which is four Pomodoros.
_1_	You have a large assignment of some sort to do.	___	After each Pomodoro, record it with a check mark.
___	If you get distracted, write it down and put them aside.	_9_	After a "set" is completed, take a longer break.
___	Complete the Pomodoro.	_6_	Take a five-minute break and do what you like.
___	Divide the assignment into smaller tasks.	___	Begin the entire process over again, as needed.

◆ Complete the Sentences

Write a sentence beginning for each sentence ending below. Use information from today's reading.

1. _____ means "tomato" in English.

2. _____ the first thing you should do is to break it down into smaller tasks.

3. _____ in the late 1980s.

4. _____ always write your ideas or thoughts down and put the paper aside until the session ends.

5. _____ using a check mark.

6. _____, because if you do not take them, your work will not be as good as it should be.

7. Make up your own ending of a sentence about today's topic.

   _____.

8. Now write the beginning of your sentence.

   _____.

◆ Discussion / Writing

I. The reading states that with the Pomodoro technique, you should work for 25 minutes and then take a five-minute break. But it also says that you can work longer or take longer breaks, depending on what best fits you and your needs. What do you think would be your best fit?

I think that for me, working for _____ minutes and then taking a

break for _____ minutes would work best. This is because _____

_____

_____ .

II. Do you think that you would be able to adapt the Pomodoro technique to your own needs and purposes? If so, how? If not, why not?

I (**think / don't think**) that I would be able to use this technique. The reason is _____

_____

_____ .

Make up some questions of your own that are related to today's reading. *Be creative!!*

5

Introverts and Extroverts

内向性と外向性

◆ Pre-Reading Question

What are some differences between introverts and extroverts?

◆ Vocabulary

1. Behavior 行動
2. Classified 分類された
3. Decisions 決定
4. Depending upon 応じて
5. Relationships 関係
6. Shallow 浅い

◆ **Fill in each blank in the sentences below with the correct word or phrase. Make sure you use the appropriate word forms.**

a. Her poor _____ made everyone dislike her.

b. I buy apples, _____ how fresh they are.

c. The couple was _____ and only cared about appearances.

d. When you make _____, consider all the options.

e. Tomatoes are not vegetables; they are _____ as fruits.

f. Ben valued the _____ he had with his friends.

31

◆ Reading 🎧 06

*"Your vision will become clear only when you can look into your own heart. Who looks outside, dreams; who looks inside, awakens." – **Carl Jung***

Take this introvert / extrovert test: Mark either "**Yes**" or "**No**" about yourself.

1. I like to complete one task at a time. _____ **2.** I am a good listener. _____ **3.** On free evenings, I enjoy relaxing at home. _____ **4.** I enjoy being by myself. _____ **5.** I think before I speak. _____ **6.** After spending time with a lot of people, I need some time alone. _____ **7.** I get nervous being around people I do not know. _____ **8.** Doing things I have never done before often gives me stress. _____ 9. I often do several things at once. _____ **10.** I like talking to many different people. _____ **11.** For me, a fun time is going out with friends. _____ **12.** When I am by myself, I often become bored. _____ **13.** I will often say things without thinking. _____ **14.** Social events excite and energize me. _____ **15.** I enjoy talking to strangers. _____ **16.** I am eager to try new, different things. _____

[1] Carl Jung was a psychologist who believed that one way we can better know ourselves, is to be aware of and understand our own attitudes and behaviors. To Jung, what appears as random behavior is actually not random at all. In 1921, he first classified people as being either introvert or extrovert.

[2] Introverts get more energy from being alone. They take the time to understand their own thoughts and feelings, and tend to look carefully within themselves before making decisions. Extroverts get their energy from being with other people and tend to focus their attention outside of themselves. They are more social and confident, and make quicker decisions.

Examples of Introvert and Extrovert Character Traits and Behaviors:

Introvert Character Traits and Behaviors: 1. Prefer spending time alone. **2.** Spending time with others lowers energy. Prefer smaller events. **3.** Are natural listeners. Very careful when speaking. **4.** Prefer doing one thing at a time. **5.** Enjoy thinking about different theories, beliefs. **6.** Can have difficulty adapting to new situations. **7.** May lose track of the outside world. **8.** When making decisions, carefully think of all options. **9.** Enjoy subjects like math, science, or history, among others. **10.** Have fewer friends but closer relationships.

Extrovert Character Traits and Behaviors: A. Very aware of what is going on outside of themselves. **B.** Tend to become bored when alone. **C.** Often make quick decisions and take risks. **D.** Prefer doing many tasks at once. **E.** Get energy from being social, and from spending time with friends and meeting new people. **F.** Get bored with classes and school. **G.** Talkative and quick to speak and express themselves. **H.** Have many friends but shallow relationships. **I.** Love trying new, different things. **J.** Quickly get bored with ideas.

[3] Jung believed that we all experience the world in different ways. Thus, it is important to have a flexible approach when we try to understand something as complex as people's

personalities. There is no right or wrong personality. And no one is completely introvert or extrovert. Rather, people are a combination of both personality types. Neither type is better. Either type can connect or form a relationship with anyone, **depending upon** the situation. This new awareness, if we use it wisely, can deepen our understanding of others and improve our relations with them.

[4] Unfortunately, we often use this self-knowledge to limit our beliefs and to classify ourselves into small boxes or fixed categories. This is unfortunate because this self-knowledge is supposed to help us better understand our own nature and character. It is supposed to show us the different ways we see and deal with the world around us. It is supposed to give us the freedom to be ourselves – to be anything we want to be – and not take that freedom away from us. Always remember, your personality is yours. We are all free to be whomever we like.

*"At the center of your being, you have the answer; you know who you are and know what you want." – **Lao Tzu***

◆ Active Outline

1. Carl Jung was a specialist in _____. **(math / English / psychology / history)**

2. Introverts get their energy from inside themselves while extroverts get their energy from outside themselves. **(True / False)**

3. Jung believed that everyone has pretty much the same type of personality. **(True / False)**

4. Unfortunately, we often use self-knowledge to _____ ourselves, while it should be used to better _____ ourselves.
   (limit, understand / understand, limit)

◆ Comprehension

Look at the list of behaviors and personality traits below. Mark "I" if it describes an Introvert and "E" if it describes an Extrovert.

a.	Has fewer friends, stronger relationships. ____	Likes being social. ____	Talkative.	____
b.	Prefers smaller groups of people. ____	Likely to take chances. ____	Takes action quickly. ____	
c.	Good at imagining something completed. ____	Confident with strangers. ____	Thoughtful.	____
d.	Has difficulty doing too much at once. ____	May appear cold to others. ____	Communicates easily.	____
e.	Likely wants power, prestige, respect. ____	Gets bored with ideas. ____	Enjoys attention.	____
f.	Likes carefully doing one thing at a time. ____	Loses track of others. ____	Prefers quiet.	____

◆ Matching

Go to the text section labeled "Examples of Introvert and Extrovert Character Traits and Behaviors." Match each Introvert Behavior with its opposing Extrovert Behavior.

1. _B_   2. ____   3. ____   4. ____   5. ____   6. _I_   7. ____   8. ____   9. ____   10. ____

◆ Grade your Introvert / Extrovert Test

For questions 1 to 8, give yourself one point for each "No" answer. For questions 9 to 16, give yourself one point for each "Yes" answer. Add up your score.

My score is ____

- ◆ (0-3) Very introverted. (4-6) Somewhat introverted. (7-9) About equally introverted and extroverted. (10-12) Somewhat extroverted. (13-16) Very extroverted.

According to the results of the test, I am more (**introverted / extroverted / a combination of both types**). I (**do / do not**) agree because _____

_____

_____ .

◆ Creative / Critical Thinking

Which of your behaviors are more introvert or more extrovert? Give examples.

Introvert	Extrovert
Ex: I prefer to spend my time alone.	I am very outgoing and love connecting with others.

1. _____   1. _____

2. _____   2. _____

> **Opinion: Do you think you would be able to switch from being an introvert to being an extrovert or from being an extrovert to being an introvert? Could you switch for a week? A month? Longer? Would you like to try? How would you go about it? Make a plan.**

If I were to switch from introvert to extrovert or extrovert to introvert for a **(week /month /** _____ **)** I would first **(do / change)** _____ _____. Then I would **(do / change)** _____ _____.

Overall, I **(do / do not)** believe that it is possible to make such a switch. This is because _____.

- ◆ **Complete the paragraph by filling in each blank with "introverts" or "extroverts" (Note: The answers are not in the text). Make sure you use the correct form (singular or plural) where needed.**

The introvert and extrovert will often misunderstand each other. The **(1)** _____ sees the **(2)** _____ as shallow, loud, and perhaps deceitful. In contrast, the **(3)** _____ sees the **(4)** _____ as dull, arrogant, and self-centered. This is not to say that the two cannot get along. In Asian countries such as China and Japan, **(5)** _____ are valued more, while in the West, **(6)** _____ are seen as well adjusted.

◆ Discussion Exercise

Tell us about a time when you were more of an introvert and about another time when you were more of an extrovert.

There have been times when I was more of an **introvert**. For example, one time _____ _____.

There have been times when I was more of an **extrovert**. For example, one time _____ _____.

Learning and knowing about these two different character types **(has / has not)** been a useful tool for understanding myself better. This is because _____

_____.

◆ Discussion / Writing

I. Would you prefer a job that is typical for introverts or extroverts? Why? Give examples.

I would prefer to have a job that is done by **(introverts / extroverts)**. This is because

_____.

For example, _____

_____.

II. Who do you think is happier, introverts or extroverts? Why?

I think that **(introverts / extroverts)** are happier. This is because _____

_____

For example, _____.

◆ Discussion / Debate

1. What do you think Jung's theory of introverts and extroverts? Did you find it interesting? True? Difficult? Boring? Did it give you a better understanding of human behavior? Why or why not?

_____

_____

_____

2. Carl Jung believed that people can be in the middle or near to one end of the introvert-extrovert scale. However, no one is a complete introvert or extrovert. Do you agree with this? Why or why not?

_____

_____

_____

Make up some questions of your own that are related to today's reading. Be creative!!

Social Media and Loneliness
SNS と孤独

◆ Pre-Reading Question

Is using social media good or bad for us? Why do you think so?

◆ Vocabulary

1. Acquaintances 知人   2. Brag 自慢   3. Compare 比較
4. Depression うつ   5. Realistic 現実的

◆ **Match the sentence beginnings with their endings.**

1. Mina would often **compare** her body style with _____   a. about his wealth.

2. Shoko had many **acquaintances** _____   b. lasted for several weeks.

3. After Mike failed the test, his **depression** _____   c. writing one short story a month.

4. Ellen set herself a **realistic** goal of _____   d. others, and it made her unhappy.

5. Mark would often **brag** _____   e. but few truly close friends.

[1] Facebook, Twitter, and all the other social media are now a huge part of our society and lives. They play such a large role, among the younger generation, that some people feel social media defines the generation. Young people today have even been labeled the social-media generation, which is not necessarily positive. In fact, some studies have shown that they are the loneliest of all current generations. And **compared** to older generations, they are more likely to have no close friends or even casual **acquaintances**. Some are said to have no friends at all.

[2] While social media is supposed to connect us all socially, studies have linked longer daily social-media usage to feelings of loneliness, general unhappiness, and even **depression**. Though it would not be **realistic** for us to stop using social media altogether, limiting the time we spend using them is a more **realistic** goal. People who cut in half their social-media use were found to be happier overall.

[3] Studies have found that the biggest problem with social media – what makes users unhappy – is that users very frequently **compare** themselves to others. There's a simple reason for this: online, people tend to exaggerate the positives in their lives. They **brag** about themselves and post only the highlights of their lives. When this happens, it is easy for us to conclude that everyone else is having more fun, doing more exciting things, and living a far better life than we are. We get the feeling that we are being left out and thus feel bad about ourselves. Experiencing these feelings day after day can cause us huge stress. We tend to **compare** what we have to what others have – their homes, their cars, their clothes, their jobs and friends. Younger females would often **compare** themselves to other females in terms of beauty and, as a result, feel less attractive – sometimes feeling so bad about themselves that they slip into **depression**.

[4] A second problem related to social-media use is that every minute we spend online could be better spent doing something much more useful, such as visiting friends, working, or having meaningful conversations. Today, we are spending less and less time in the company of others and more and more time online – around two and a half hours a day on average. This number

is increasing every year. Some people spend more time online than they do sleeping.

[5] Research has also found that the best way to use social media is as a tool to improve our relationships and to create more meaningful, deeper connections. Social media are, of course, a handy way to keep in contact with friends and family who are far away. But sadly, when our only "friends" are online, they do little to relieve our loneliness. What this means, then, is that it is important that we use social media as a tool to improve our normal, face-to-face relationships, and not as a replacement for meeting friends.

*"Comparison is the death of joy." – **Mark Twain***

◆ Active Outline

1. Today's younger generation is often called the _____ generation.
   (social-media / friendliest / happiest)

   a. Today's _____ generation is said to be the loneliest. **(younger / oldest)**

2. Many studies have linked social-media use to _____.
   (loneliness / being social)

   a. It _____ realistic for us to stop using social media altogether. **(is / is not)**

   b. Those who have _____ their social media use are happier. **(stopped / limited)**

3. Users of social-media _____ compare themselves to others. **(seldom / frequently)**

   a. Unfortunately, social-media users often post what _____ really happening in their real lives. **(is / is not)**

   b. Younger women who see more attractive women online often feel _____ about themselves. **(better / worse)**

4. People today waste a lot of time _____ instead of doing something more useful.
   (visiting friends / doing homework / having face-to-face conversations / being online)

   a. Some people spend more time online than they do sleeping. **(True / False)**

5. Social media are best used _____.
   (on Facebook / on Twitter / with other apps / to keep in contact with family and friends)

◆ Critical / Creative Thinking

List two advantages and two disadvantages of social media. (Note: The answers are not in the today's reading.)

Advantages	Disadvantages
1. _____	1. _____
2. _____	2. _____

Opinion: **Overall, do you think that using social media makes you feel lonely? Explain.**

◆ Word Scramble

Unscramble the words to make complete sentences. After you finish, decide if each sentence is True or False.

1. more likely to / generation is / have lots of friends / and acquaintances. / The social-media

_____ **True / False**

2. media have been / unhappiness. / feelings of / Social / linked to

_____ **True / False**

3. what they see / People tend to compare / on social media / they themselves have. / to what

_____ **True / False**

4. media decreases. / the number of / Every year / on social / hours people spend

_____ **True / False**

5. current relationships. / replace your / be used / Social media should / as a tool to

_____ **True / False**

◆ Word Fill

Fill in each blank in the two paragraphs below with the word that best completes the sentence's main idea. Complete the final sentence in each paragraph on your own.

Paragraph 1

Researchers have found that compared to _____ generations, today's young people, at times called the _____ _____ generation, are the _____ of all previous generations. This loneliness could be due to all the time they spend on _____ _____. Research also shows, however, that people who limit their social-media use are overall _____. In my opinion, limiting my use of social media **(will / will not)** make me happier. This is because _____
_____.

Paragraph 2

According to researchers, the biggest problem with social media is that while using them, people tend to _____ themselves to others. When young women compare themselves with other _____ who the young women feel are more attractive, they feel _____ about themselves. People are spending more and more time online, and every year this number is _____. Experts say that the best way to use social media is as a tool for improving our existing _____. In my opinion, I **(agree / do not agree)** with this idea. This is because _____
_____.

◆ Discussion / Writing

Write brief answers to these questions, and then discuss them.

I. **How big a role do social media play in your life? Does using social media cause you stress or make you less social? Explain.**

_____
_____
_____

II. **Do you find that others exaggerate or brag about themselves on social media to make themselves look better? Do you ever do this? Explain.**

_____
_____
_____

III. If you could go back to a time when there were no such things as Facebook and other social media, would you? Why or why not?

_____

_____

_____

◆ Debate

1. Do you think social media are a source of good for people or society? Or, is it a kind of poison for our culture that is turning people into a bunch of robots? Explain.

_____

_____

_____

2. Overall, do you agree with the ideas expressed in today's reading? Why or why not?

_____

_____

_____

Make up some questions of your own that are related to today's reading. _Be creative!!_

Five Healthy Habits

5 つの健康的な習慣

◆ Pre-Reading Question

What are some good habits that will keep you healthier and extend your life?

◆ Vocabulary

1. Destroy 破壊　　2. Emotional health 情緒的健康　　3. Obvious 明らか

4. Prevented 防止　　5. Priority 優先順位　　6. Range 範囲

◆ **Fill in each blank in the sentences below with the correct word or phrase.**

a. Her singing voice had a _____ that went from low to high.

b. Wearing a seatbelt had _____ injury.

c. If we work too hard, we may _____ our physical and
_____.

d. For good grades, make studying a top _____.

e. How to fix the problem quickly was _____ to everyone except the
boss.

◆ Reading 🎧 08

"It's not the years in your life that count, it's the life in your years."
– Abraham Lincoln

[1] A health study done at Harvard University in 2018 followed some 120,000 people for more than three decades. The study found that keeping five simple healthy daily habits could extend a person's life from ten to fifteen years, or more. The study's subjects who faithfully practiced these five habits **prevented** many medical issues – from heart disease to cancer – and greatly improved their quality of life.

[2] Maintain a healthy diet: Perhaps the most essential habit of all is to eat healthy, nutritious foods. It's easy to eat a cheeseburger or some other fast food on your way to or from school or work. However, eating too much fast or junk food is not only unhealthy – it's downright dangerous. The key to a healthy diet is to limit your processed and fried foods as well as red meat and sugary sweets, and to stick to natural foods such as grains, fruits, vegetables, eggs, fish, and nuts. One recent study found that one in five deaths worldwide are linked to a poor diet. So, by all means, watch what you eat!

[3] Daily exercise: It goes without saying that sitting around all day is bad for us. So another important habit to form is to make daily exercise a top **priority**. Exercising for just thirty minutes a day can work miracles – and greatly extend your life. You do not have to go to the gym, or lift heavy weights, or actively play a sport. All you need to do is to take a brisk 30-minute walk every day. Even doing something as simple as working in the garden

regularly can help keep you in good shape. If you haven't exercised for a while, begin slowly. After just a month or so of steady exercise, you will find yourself naturally – automatically – eating better, sleeping more soundly, losing weight, having more energy, and feeling happier all around.

[4] Maintain a healthy weight: A proper or healthy weight varies from person to person, so find out what yours is and make every effort to keep it within the proper **range**. Remember: Being underweight can be as unhealthy as being overweight. Maintaining a healthy weight puts less stress on the body. It allows you to get a better night's sleep and improves your **emotional health**. So what is the "trick" to proper weight management? You guessed it: Maintaining a healthy diet and getting regular exercise.

[5] Limit your alcohol: Alcohol is everywhere, and it's all right to have an occasional drink. But, as in all things, don't overdo it. Excessive consumption of alcohol leads to a host of problems: weight gain, serious illness, alcoholic addiction, and a shorter life. So when you do have to go out for a drink, limit yourself to just a drink or two at most.

[6] Don't smoke: No matter how healthy your diet or how regularly you exercise, if you smoke, you are putting yourself at risk. Smoking can **destroy** every organ in your body. To put it more bluntly, smoking kills, leading to the deaths of one in ten people worldwide. So if you don't smoke now, don't start. If you do smoke, stop. The good news is that more and more people everywhere have gotten the "Don't smoke!" message. Smoking is on the decline. And good riddance.

[7] Forming and sticking to these good health habits is up to each of us. Though their benefits may seem **obvious**, maintaining them in everyday life is not always easy. But as we learned in Lesson 3, forming and sticking to good habits can be done. So if you haven't already made these five good health habits a part of your life, by all means do so. You will give yourself the gift of a longer healthier, happier life.

"To me, the surprising outcome was how strong it was: what a big impact these simple behaviors could have on life expectancy."
– Dr. Meir Stampfer, co-author of the study.

◆ Active Outline

1. The Harvard study found that keeping five healthy habits can _____ your life.
   (shorten / extend)

2. For a healthy diet, you should stick to natural foods such as fruits and vegetables.
   (True / False)

3. Exercise should be a priority _____. **(weekly / daily / monthly)**

4. A person's healthy weight range varies from _____.
   (day to day / one person to the next)

5. It is all right to drink alcohol _____. **(often / occasionally / never)**

6. You should _____ smoke cigarettes. **(often / occasionally / never)**

7. Following all of these five habits _____ always easy to do. **(is / is not)**

45

◆ Comprehension

Fill in each blank to complete the sentences below.

1. The study completed at Harvard University followed over _____ people for over _____ decades.
   (100,000, five / 80,000, two / 175,000, seven / 120,000, three)

2. People who followed these five habits _____.
   (had a better quality of life / lived longer / both of these / neither of these)

3. Exercise can include _____.
   (walking / gardening / going to the gym / all of these)

4. Soda _____ a natural food. **(is / is not)**

5. Each of these healthy habits _____ within our power to form and stick to.
   (is / is not)

◆ Critical Thinking

Rank the five healthy habits from *the easiest to the most difficult* for you to follow. Give a brief reason why.

	Habit	A Brief Reason Why
Easiest	_____	_____
Fairly Easy	_____	_____
Medium	_____	_____
Difficult	_____	_____
Most Difficult	_____	_____

> Opinion: **Which of these habits are you following now? Which are you not following? Explain.**

◆ Matching

Based on today's reading, match the sentence beginnings and endings.

1. One study found five habits that could ( )
2. You should avoid fast foods ( )
3. I spend around eight hours a day sitting, ( )
4. After I began exercising, I could sleep better ( )
5. It is important to maintain a healthy weight, ( )
6. Be careful not to drink too much ( )
7. Smoking is extremely dangerous ( )
8. These habits are within your control ( )

a. … but never realized how unhealthy it was.
b. … when you go to a party.
c. … but following all of them is not easy.
d. … even when you are in a hurry.
e. … extend one's life by over a decade.
f. … and had more energy.
g. … and can destroy every organ in your body.
h. … that is, not to be too heavy or too skinny.

◆ Discussion / Writing

I. The article lists five habits that can extend your life. Think of four additional habits that can also help to keep you healthy.

A. _____   B. _____

C. _____   D. _____

II. In your opinion, what are two healthy habits that are not mentioned in today's reading that are important in keeping you healthy and making you happier? Why do you think these habits are so important?

The two habits I can think of to help make me healthier and happier that are not

in the reading are (1) _____ and (2) _____. I think these habits

are important because _____

_____.

Opinion: Have you been able to form or follow these habits yourself? Explain.

III. What did you find most informative in today's reading? Explain.

What I found most informative was _____

_____.

◆ Debate

Overall, do you agree with the ideas expressed in today's reading? Why or why not?

_____

_____

_____

Make up some questions of your own that are related to today's reading. Be creative!!

Are Humans Outdated Machines? Part I

人間は時代遅れの機械？ Part 1

◆ Pre-Reading Question

It has been said that humans are outdated machines. Do you agree or disagree? Explain.

◆ Vocabulary:

1. Ancient 古代
2. Emotional 感情的
3. Instincts 本能
4. Outdated 時代遅れ
5. Overreact 過剰反応
6. Survival 生き残り
7. Threat 脅威

◆ Match the words with their meanings or descriptions.

a. _____ Something that causes fear or danger.

b. _____ Something from the very distant past.

c. _____ Ability to stay alive.

d. _____ Expressed with feeling.

e. _____ Natural behavior; drive; impulse.

f. _____ No longer new; old fashioned.

g. _____ To respond to something too strongly.

◆ Reading 🎧 09

*"The saddest aspect of life right now is that science gathers knowledge faster than society gathers wisdom." – **Isaac Asimov***

[1] Today, with all our airplanes and cars, our cellphones and the Internet, our GPS and smart TV sets, the world has become a very modern, high-tech, and – in a way – a much smaller place. But the fact is, we humans haven't really caught up to this new world. We are still more adapted to living in the world as it was tens of thousands of years ago, when it was a scary place indeed. Back then we were afraid of snakes, spiders, rats, sharks, and countless other natural threats (as most of us today still are!). Yet now, in this modern age, we have no fear of automobiles, for example, which kill more people than all those natural dangers put together.

[2] Imagine for a second that you are at a party with many people. Out of nowhere, someone becomes angry with you for something you did not do – shouting for no reason at all. You become troubled. Your heart beats faster; your hands begin to sweat. You start shouting back at the person. Before you even knew what was happening – or even if there was a real threat – your feelings jumped in, in ways that you may later regret. You ask yourself: Why did I see that person as a threat? Why did I feel the need to respond so quickly – and so angrily?

[3] The answer to that is simply because the human brain is still adapted to life as it was tens of thousands of years ago. Our brain is physically still very similar to what it was back then; it behaves as if it is still living in those ancient times. Back then, we faced countless dangers – real ones. In those ancient times, feeling fear was essential to survival. It allowed us to take action to protect ourselves. In this regard, ancient humans were much like today's wild animals.

[4] The human brain has two parts: the emotional brain and the thinking brain. The emotional brain is the older, deeper part – the one that allows us to react to threats and survive. We rarely use this part today – only when we feel very strong emotions or must react to something very quickly. Say you come upon an emergency or accident of some sort. Someone is in real danger, and you must react right away, almost without thinking about it. That's where the emotional brain comes in. We also use it when playing sports, as then someone suddenly throws a ball at us and we must react quickly, either to catch it or to avoid getting hit by it. The emotional brain also comes into play when we cry. A thought arises there and then quickly moves to the thinking part of the brain, which serves us well enough for most of our daily activities. It allows us to plan ahead, reason, reflect on experience, and figure out how things work.

[5] It has been said that we humans are outdated machines. And in the sense explained above, we are. This ancient part of the brain still affects our understanding of the world we live in. The stress that other people cause us is no longer a real threat to our survival. But our "old-fashioned" brain acts as if it is. In fact, it often overreacts and creates more stress than we need for self-protection – for survival. No matter how smart, sophisticated, and modern

we have become, the **instincts** we had from those tens of thousands of years ago are still there within us, influencing our behavior. So the next time you **overreact** to something, the next time you become unnecessarily angry or sad, try to remember how the **outdated** brain affects your responses to so many situations.

*"To enjoy good health, to bring happiness to one's family, to bring peace to all, one must first discipline and control one's own mind." – **The Buddha***

◆ Active Outline

1. Humans are still more adapted to living _____.
   (today / 50 years ago / tens of thousands of years ago)

   a. _____ are more dangerous to people than all other threats combined.
      (Snakes / Spiders / Sharks / Cars)

2. At times, we see other people as a threat, when they actually are not. **(True / False)**

3. The brain is very _____ the way it was tens of thousands of years ago.
   (different from / similar to)

4. The emotional part of the brain is the _____ part of the brain. **(older / newer)**

   a. Thousands of years ago, when an animal attacked us, it would have been the _____ brain that protected us. **(emotional / thinking / modern / inward)**

   b. A thought begins in the _____ part of the brain and then moves to the _____ part of the brain.
      (emotional, thinking / thinking, emotional / inside, outside / outside, inside)

   c. Today, for most activities, we use the _____ part of the brain.
      (emotional / thinking / modern)

5. The brain generally creates stress in us to protect us if there is a _____.
   (friend / car / threat)

   a. Our brain is very much outdated, and yet today can still affect how we react. **(True / False)**

◆ Comprehension

Use information from today's reading to fill in the gaps.

1. We live in a very ___modern___, high-tech world, and yet we are more adapted to life as it was lived _____ ago. Back then, humans lived in fear of _____, and many of us still do. Yet have no fear of _____, which kill far more people than any of those natural threats.

2. The human brain has two parts, the older, _____ brain and the deeper, _____ brain. The emotional brain was important for allowing us to act very **(slowly / carefully / quickly)** in the face of danger. It made _____ possible. In today's world, the emotional brain can be used for, say, playing _____. The newer "thinking" part of the brain, on the other hand, is used for _____. But no matter how _____ we become, those natural _____ from all those thousands of years ago are still there influencing our behavior.

3. Unfortunately, the human brain is more adapted to the world of the _____ than it is to the world of _____. It is the _____ part of the brain that often takes over in certain situations. It may create more _____ than necessary, which **(is / is not)** a problem. In most situations, we use the _____ part of the brain; however, even the most intelligent people **(can / cannot)** always overcome their ancient instincts. This could explain why, when we are at a party, for example, and someone becomes _____ with us for no good reason, we may overreact in ways that we later _____.

◆ Critical / Creative Thinking

What parts of the reading do you agree with, disagree with, or have doubts about?

Agree	Disagree / Doubt
1._____	1._____
2._____	2._____
3._____	3._____

> Opinion: **Overall, do you agree or disagree with the ideas expressed in today's reading? Why?**

Overall I (**agree / disagree**) with the article. This is because _____

_____.

◆ Agree or Disagree?

Read these statements and circle "agree" or "disagree." Explain your reasons.

1. Most people get angry from time to time, yet later cannot explain why and regret having become so angry.

   I (**agree / disagree**) with this because _____

   _____.

2. Older people have better control over their emotions than younger people.

   I (**agree / disagree**) with this because _____

   _____.

3. In today's modern world, the emotional brain is no longer important.

   I (**agree / disagree**) with this because _____

   _____.

4. I believe that it is possible to control the emotional brain.

   I (**agree / disagree**) with this because _____

   _____.

5. I feel that this information about people and their emotional brain is important to know.

   I (**agree / disagree**) with this because _____

   _____.

6. Make up and write your own "Agree or Disagree?" sentence here.

   _____

   I (**agree / disagree**) with this because _____

   _____.

◆ Discussion / Writing

I. Give examples of when the emotional brain is more important and useful.

The emotional brain is more important _____

_____

_____.

II. Give examples of when the thinking brain is more important and useful.

The thinking brain is more important _____

_____

_____.

III. Sometimes, our brain will mistake an emotional threat for a physical threat. How would you deal with such a situation?

_____

_____

_____

Make up some questions of your own that are related to today's reading. Be creative!!

9

Are Humans Outdated Machines? Part II: Controlling Stress

人間は時代遅れの機械？ Part 2：ストレスの制御

◆ **Pre-Reading Question**

When we feel threatened or afraid, how can we control our stress? Explain.

◆ **Vocabulary**:

> 1. Inappropriate 不適切
> 2. Psychological 心理学
> 3. Sensible 賢明な
> 4. Threatened 脅迫

◆ **Fill in each blank in the sentences below with the correct word.**

a. Yu Lin felt _____ when another passenger on the train began glaring at her.

b. After his parents got divorced, it may have caused some _____ problems.

c. Be _____! Don't be in such a hurry! Think before you act!

d. When the speaker used an _____ word, some audience members walked out.

◆ Reading 🎧10

"Thou shalt not make a machine in the likeness of a human mind."
— Orange Catholic Bible, Dune, Frank Herbert

[1] As we learned in our last lesson, we humans are, in one sense at least, better suited to life as it was lived some tens of thousands of years ago. Back then, because of the many **threats** of death and destruction in the natural environment, our emotional brain often took charge of our behavior, allowing us to make life-saving decisions. When an animal **threatened** to attack us, we had to think and act quickly. If we didn't, we soon became the animal's dinner. And humanity would not have survived.

[2] In today's world, however, there are far fewer such physical threats. But there are plenty of **psychological** ones. Whether we feel **threatened** physically or **psychologically**, though, the emotional part of our brain reacts the same way as it did tens of thousands of years ago. It often still sees and judges threats as physical.

[3] In stressful situations of all kinds, our emotions take over and determine our response. The emotional part of the brain is deeper inside the brain and controls our strongest emotions: anger, fear, sadness, disgust, hatred. That's why when we feel **threatened**, we often can't think clearly or control our reactions. The body responds with the heart racing faster, sudden sweating, sharpened vision, and increased strength, all of which cause us to overreact. And when we do, the emotional brain takes charge. The thinking, **sensible** part of the brain is set off to the side, and we lose control of ourselves and make bad decisions.

[4] What can we do to prevent such **inappropriate** reactions? When you feel a **threat** of some sort, make every effort to keep calm and maintain control. Take deep breaths. Allow some time to bring your thinking brain forward and make good use of it, so that you can make thoughtful, **sensible**, appropriate decisions. One thing you should never do is to judge yourself as being good or bad. To remain calm and **sensible** can be difficult, and it takes lots of patience and practice. It does help to remember, however, that you are not alone: What is happening to you happens to everyone.

[5] Today's modern world is filled with tensions of all kinds. Our relations and dealings with family, classmates, and colleagues can cause us serious stress. As constant news of natural disasters and wars and mysterious new diseases spread around the globe, it make us feel deeply uneasy and even frightened. And, as we have learned, we can still react emotionally to these **psychological** stresses just as we responded to physical **threats** from ancient times. But you should always try hard not to. Instead, think of each situation in the most realistic, **sensible** way. When confronted with an emotional event. Stop. Wait. Count to ten. Those extra few moments will allow your thinking brain to take charge and help you find the best way to deal with the situation and come up with a **sensible** solution.

"What we are born with is what worked best for the last 50,000 human generations, not the last 500 generations – and certainly not the last five."–**Daniel Goleman**

◆ Active Outline

1. When an animal attacked a person thousands of years ago, it was the _____ brain that protected us. **(emotional / thinking)**

2. In today's world, we have far more _____ threats than _____ threats. **(physical, psychological / psychological, physical)**

3. The _____ part of the brain is deeper than the _____ part.
   (emotional, thinking / thinking, emotional)

   a. When we react too quickly to a threat, the thinking part of the brain is put to the side and we often make _____ decisions. **(good / great / poor)**

4. When faced with a difficult situation, we should first of all _____.
   (stress out / react quickly / use our emotional brain / wait)

   a. One way to control our reactions to what we think is a threat is to _____.
   (judge ourselves harshly / have an inappropriate reaction / calm down / react quickly)

   b. Reactions like these happen to _____. **(only you / everybody but you / everybody)**

5. We are prone to respond to today's psychological stresses in _____ we responded to physical threats thousands of years ago. **(a different way than / the same way as)**

   a. The best way to respond to these problems is to use your _____ brain.
   (emotional / thinking / artistic / tiny)

◆ Article Summary

Which of these headlines offers the best summary of today's reading?

a. Human beings' poor brains lead to poor decisions.

b. Controlling stress and inappropriate reactions in the modern world.

c. The emotional brain versus the intelligent brain.

d. Humans are better suited to life tens of thousands of years ago.

◆ Word Scramble

Unscramble the words to make complete sentences.

1. psychological / today / Most threats / than physical. / are more

   _____

2. reaction, slow down / inappropriate / and relax. / To prevent / an

   _____

3. of our emotions / stress, why do we / When we feel / lose control / quickly / choices? / and make poor

   _____

4. quick decisions / had to make / humans / Thousands of years ago, / emotional brain. / using their

   _____

5. sensible / to take charge. / by allowing / brain / We can find / solutions / our thinking

   _____

◆ Sentence Matching

Match the unscrambled sentences above with the paragraphs in today's reading in which the sentence's information can be found.

Paragraph 1. Sentence: _____   **Paragraph 2.** Sentence: _____

Paragraph 3. Sentence: _____   **Paragraph 4.** Sentence: _____

Paragraph 5. Sentence: _____

◆ Reverse Questions

Write the questions that you would need to ask to get the answers below.

1. **Question:** Over 50,000 years ago, _____

   _____?

   Answer: No, at that time there were far more physical than psychological threats.

2. **Question:** What happens to people when _____

   _____?

   Answer: When this happens, they sweat, have sharper vision, and their hearts beat faster.

3. **Question:** Which part of the brain _____

   _____?

   Answer: When we react too quickly, it is the emotional part of the brain that takes control.

4. **Question:** When the emotional part _____

   _____?

   Answer: When this happens, we respond without thinking and often overreact and make poor decisions.

5. **Question:** In threatening situations, what _____

   _____?

   Answer: The most important thing is to calm down and find a thoughtful, sensible solution.

6. **Question:** Which part of the brain _____

   _____?

   Answer: We should use the thinking part of the brain when we feel a psychological threat.

◆ Discussion / Writing

Write brief answers to the questions below. Then share your ideas with a partner.

I. **What occupations require the emotional brain more? How about the thinking brain? Explain why.**

_____

_____

_____

II. Think of a time when you felt that your emotional brain had taken over and you acted inappropriately. What happened?

_____

_____

_____

III. What is your best technique for controlling yourself and calming down in a stressful situation?

_____

_____

_____

IV. What are you feeling stressed about right now?

_____

_____

_____

V. White a short paragraph in which you relate the ideas and information in today's reading to your own experiences, perhaps with things that have happened to you or decisions that you have made. Then share your paragraph's story with a partner.

_____

_____

_____

◆ Debate

Was today's reading of any practical value to you? Did you find the information and advice in it useful? On a scale of 1 to 10 (10 being highest), rate the reading's usefulness to you. Be honest! Write a short paragraph in which you explain your rating. Then share your ideas with a classmate whose rating is much higher or lower than yours.

On a scale of 1 to 10, for me this article has a practical value of _____.
This is because _____

_____.

Make up some questions of your own that are related to today's reading. _Be creative!!_

10

The Happiness Set Point
幸福の設定値

◆ Pre-Reading Question

Can we boost our level of happiness? How much control do we have over our happiness? Express it in a percentage.

◆ Vocabulary

1. Adapt 適応
2. Behavior 行動
3. Circumstances 生活環境
4. Control コントロール
5. Genetic 遺伝学
6. Remain 残り
7. Steady 安定した

◆ **Fill in each blank in the sentences below with the correct word. Make sure you use the appropriate word forms.**

a. At first, some students' _____ was hurtful to the rest of the class. However, in time, they _____ to the class, and from then on, and throughout the rest of the year, they were in _____ of their actions and were pleasant to be around.

b. Angela's happiness levels are based on the _____ that she received from her parents. Since she comes from poor _____ growing up was challenging, and she had a hard time keeping her happiness level _____, but she always _____ optimistic.

◆ Reading 🎧11

"Happiness is not something ready-made. It comes from your own actions."
– Dalai Lama

[1] The Happiness Set Point is a theory that our overall level of happiness **remains steady** throughout our lives. No matter what happens, good or bad, our level of happiness will go up or down for only short periods of time. However, after we always somehow **adapt** and then return to our normal or "set point" level of happiness. It makes no difference what it is – be it money, success, or health, or the lack thereof – causes these up and down periods of happiness or unhappiness.

[2] The Happiness Set Point is our normal level of happiness. It is estimated to be a combination of 50 percent **genetics**, 10 percent life **circumstances**, and the **remaining** 40 percent is something that we ourselves have **control** over. We are born with our **genetic** make-up, so we can't change it. Life **circumstance** is what we are born into, and may include such things as our wealth, health, social position, and where we live – all have strong **control** over our lives and happiness. But that still leaves us with 40 percent of our level of happiness that we can **control**. Controlling these happiness levels is easier said than done, but it can be accomplished by making the right life choices with the daily decisions that we make. These can include **behaving** well, doing meaningful work, and creating and improving our relations with people whom we care about.

[3] While some events or life changes can cause us short-term unhappiness or sadness, while others can lift us to happiness or even extreme joy. But according to the theory, we always **adapt** to them, and over time return to our original state. When something good happens – like a refreshing walk through a beautiful natural landscape, buying something nice, or attending a wonderful concert – we feel truly great for a while. When something bad happens – like getting a bad grade or your beloved pet dies – we feel "down" for a certain length of time. But in the end, we again adapt and return to our normal level of happiness, which, in the long run, **remains** the same.

[4] The "set point" idea is also useful for describing things other than happiness, things like health, stress, personality, **behaviors**, and love. Take skiing as a simple example. At first, we

begin on the smallest, least challenging hills. And even this gives us a great thrill. Over time, however, the thrill evens out, so to speak. It doesn't satisfy us, or quite make us as happy. So what do we do? We adapt and after need to "up our game." To experience that same initial thrill, we need to move up to the next level – until eventually we are skiing the most challenging hill on the mountain.

"For there is nothing either good or bad, but thinking makes it so."– **Shakespeare**

◆ Active Outline

1. The Happiness Set Point theory states that one's happiness level over the long term will overall _____.

   (remain steady / go up and then down / not adapt)

   a. People _____ adapt to what happens, whether it is good or bad.

   (will / sometimes / never)

2. The Happiness Set Point is at the same level for each person. **(True / False)**

   a. What percentage of our happiness do we have some control over?
   (10% / 40% / 50% / 100%)

3. Overall, happiness levels _____ return to their normal set point levels.

   (will / will not)

4. The "set point" idea can also be used to describe stress levels, health matters, and some personality traits. **(True / False)**

◆ Comprehension

Based on today's reading, decide whether the information below is True (T), False (F), or Not Given (NG).

1. Our life circumstances are totally in our control. _____

2. It is possible to make ourselves happier by eating lots of sweets. _____

3. Dogs and cats also have a "happiness set point" that they return to. _____

4. If something sad or even tragic happens to us, we become unhappy for a while, but eventually we adapt and return to our happiness set point. _____

5. It is believed that genetics determines 50% of our happiness. _____

6. Living with too much stress can eventually harm our health. _____

7. Buying expensive items allows us to permanently increase our happiness set point. _____

8. One example of a life circumstance is being born into a particular culture. _____

◆ Critical Thinking

Two years after the event happened, which of these people do you think was happier, (1) the person who won the lottery, or (2) the person who was permanently disabled in an accident of some kind? Why? Circle the more appropriate answer in the passage below.

[1] Many people believe that one of the 1. (happiest / worst) things that can happen to a person is winning the lottery, while the 2. (happiest / worst) thing that can happen is becoming permanently disabled. According to the Happiness Set Point theory, overall, our long-term happiness levels 3. (change / do not change) much when we briefly feel either 4. (happier / unhappier / happier or unhappier). People will 5. (eventually / never) adapt to their situation, and their happiness levels 6. (will / will not) return to normal. Immediately after winning the lottery, the winner had a 7. (temporary / permanent) increase in happiness level. Winning the lottery is 8. (genetics / life circumstance / in our control). But after two years, the winner was 9. (about 10% / not much / less) happier than before winning the lottery. People who were disabled in an accident, on the other hand, had great 10. (happiness / unhappiness) at first. But after two years, these accident victims 11. (had / had not) adapted to their situation and were not as 12. (happy / unhappy) as expected. Being disabled is something that 13. (is genetic / is related to life circumstances / we can control), and this accounts for a loss of only 14. (50% / 10% / 40%) of the disabled person's level of happiness.

[2] It was found that after two years, the person who 15. (won the lottery / was disabled) was surprisingly, on average, 16. (quite a lot / only a little) happier than the other person.

◆ Comprehension

Today's reading claims that 40% of the happiness or sadness is within our control. This means that we can choose to do things that make us either happy or unhappy. List three things that make you happy and three things that make you sad.

Happy _____   _____   _____

Sad _____   _____   _____

> **Opinion:** Choose one of these items. What happened? Relate your "story" to today's reading.

One thing I did that I (**did / did not**) enjoy and that made me (**happy / sad**) was

_____. This took place in the month of

_____ in the year _____. What happened was that

_____

_____.

The (**best / worst**) part of this experience was _____

_____.

At the time, I felt great (**happiness / sadness**) for (**several hours / _____ days

/ _____ weeks / _____ months / _____**). I expected my happiness

level to return to normal (**and after a while it did / but it never did**).

◆ Discussion / Writing

I. Do you agree that our happiness "set point" remains roughly the same throughout our lives? Explain.

_____

_____

_____

II. Do you think that different countries or cultures have different happiness set points? If so, why do you think this is? If not, why not?

_____

_____

_____

III. Overall, do you agree with the ideas presented in today's reading? Why or why not?

_____

_____

_____

Make up some questions of your own that are related to today's reading. Be creative!!

The Hedonic Treadmill, Part I

ヘドニックトレッドミル Part 1

◆ Pre-Reading Question

Does having a lot of nice, expensive possessions make you happy? Explain.

◆ Vocabulary

1. Adapt 適応
2. Experience 経験
3. Luxury 贅沢
4. Permanent 永続
5. Taken for granted 当たり前の

◆ **Fill in each blank in the sentences below with the correct word or phrase.**

a. Riding his bicycle in the mountains was so much fun that Dave wanted to _____ it again.

b. The winters are cold, but I'm sure you will soon _____ and get used to them.

c. After getting a raise, the first thing Tom bought was a _____ two-million-yen Swiss watch.

d. Not long ago, the smart phone was considered amazing, but today it is _____ and a necessity.

e. The fire did _____ damage to the roof of a famous church.

◆ Reading 🎧 12

"The most important things in life aren't things." – **Anthony J. D'Angelo**

[1] The word "hedonic" can be defined as relating to pleasure. The "hedonic treadmill" is a term created in 1971. It refers to the belief that our levels of happiness will (see previous lesson) rise or fall along with the life changes that we experience, whether for better or for worse. Those happiness levels will, however, eventually return back to the level that is normal for us. What drives the treadmill is our constant desire to possess more and better things. As we acquire more money, our wants and needs increase, and we yearn for more "stuff." As the years go by, the more things we own or possess, the more we desire. We purchase ever-newer and ever-nicer things. We rush out and buy the latest item, one that is superior to – and more costly than – the one we now have. If the goods we own are cheaper and of lower quality than those our friends and neighbors have, it has a way of making us feel like failures, right?

[2] But according to the hedonic treadmill idea, purchasing newer and better stuff does not actually make us happier, at least not for very long. Why? Simply because we soon adapt and get used to the new, luxury item. It becomes our new normal – and a dull one at that. It is exactly like being on a treadmill: Running in the same spot forever, but never getting anywhere.

[3] Of course, after we get or buy our new "amazing" jacket or car or yacht, we feel happy – at first. We experience this feeling of joy. But the feeling lasts just a short time. Soon, we begin to see the new item as not good enough, as less than we want or need, and not nearly as satisfying as we thought it would be. And before long, that original sense of joy is gone, and our happiness level returns to where it first began.

[4] These changes are often so gradual that we barely notice them. But sooner or later, over the next few weeks or months, that luxury item is taken for granted. We don't see it as a luxury item after all. It soon becomes a necessity. That's how the hedonic treadmill moves. As we get job promotions and earn a higher salary and our wealth increases; as we acquire higher-quality clothes, more expensive jewelry, larger, more high-tech TV sets, and more luxury cars, our happiness level goes up for a while but then always drops back to "normal." And before we know it, we want, need, can't do without some other thing and step back on the treadmill. The sad truth is that no item – however "high-end" or

expensive – gives us long-term, permanent satisfaction or happiness.

[5] This does not mean, of course, that we should never purchase or possess nice things. It doesn't imply that wanting and acquiring those things is bad in any way. But we should keep in mind that most of us overemphasize the importance of owning and having luxury things. We should never forget that once we step on the hedonic treadmill, we might never be able to get off.

"Even if you don't have all the things you want, be grateful for the things you don't have that you don't want." – **Bob Dylan, (Chronicles 1)**

◆ Active Outline

1. People quickly adapt to _____ changes in their lives.
   (good / bad / both good and bad)

   a. After we start earning more money and acquire more wealth, we will likely to _____.
      (want more / want less / become satisfied)

2. When you buy a nice, luxury item, you _____ become happier – for a while.
   (will / will not)

   a. However, as time goes on, that expensive luxury item you just bought will _____ begin to seem normal to you. **(most likely / not)**

3. And eventually, your happiness level will _____ where it first began.
   (become greater than / become less than / return to)

4. The changes in our feelings about the things we own usually happen very _____.
   (quickly / gradually)

   a. But those luxury items give you _____ happiness.
      (temporary / permanent)

5. We should never purchase anything nice. **(True / False)**

◆ Comprehension

1. Once we step on the treadmill, getting off is easy. (**True / False**)

2. When you purchase a high-tech television, in a few years when you get another, you will likely want a set that is of _____ quality. (**higher / lower / the same**)

3. The second paragraph says that being on a "treadmill" is like running in the same spot forever and not getting anywhere. What does this statement mean to you?

   What that statement means to me is _____

   _____

   _____ .

◆ Critical Thinking (Note that the answers are not directly in the article.)

Which of these do you think would make you overall happier over a long period of time: (a) experiencing a few, large, positive changes and doing really fun, amazing activities, or (b) experiencing many small but important successes? Select the appropriate word choice. Then complete the final sentence in your own words.

When something positive happens to people, they eventually **1. (will / will not)** adapt and return to their normal level of happiness. That's why it **2. (is / is not)** important for us to make changes in our lives often to keep things fresh and to prevent boredom. Research shows that over a longer period of time, people who are happier experience **3. (many smaller changes / a few large positive changes)**, which tends to keep life new and interesting. The reason for this is, when we **4. (often / seldom / never)** try new or different things, these **5. (smaller, steadier / larger, less frequent)** changes make us happier. Therefore, for us to be happier over the long term, it is best for us to set **6. (frequent smaller / a few larger)** goals.

I **(agree / don't agree)** with this idea because _____

_____

_____

_____ .

◆ Discussion / Writing

Complete the paragraphs below.

I. When have you purchased a nice, new item and, at first, were really happy with it, but then, before long, you became used to it and eventually it was taken for granted?

About _____ (months / years / _____)

ago, I purchased (clothes / a sports item / a toy / _____). It

was a _____. When I first purchased it,

I felt _____ .

As time went on, around a month or two later, I felt _____

_____ .

Later on, _____ (months / years / _____)

after, I felt that the item _____

_____

_____ .

> **Opinion:** Have you had more satisfaction from buying a nice, new item than actually it? Explain. (For example: How many of the clothes that you own do you actually wear?)

_____

_____

_____ .

II. Give an example of when and how you can get more satisfaction from buying an item than actually using it. You can use a real example from your own experience or make up a "fictional" story using your imagination.

A while ago, I (**had a hobby / played / wanted to improve /**_____)
my _____. So, I got a new _____.
However, I soon wanted to upgrade again and get (**a new /
another / a better**) _____. While this was all right, the
_____ also needed improvement. And as I was
there, I also wanted to (**improve / get another**) _____
_____
_____.

III. How about you? Do you think that owning a lot of new, luxury items can make people happy? Why or why not?

I (**do / do not**) think that owning such things makes us happier. This is because
_____
_____
_____.

Make up some questions of your own that are related to today's reading. Be creative!!

12

The Hedonic Treadmill Part II:
Can We Control It?

ヘドニックトレッドミル Part 2: 制御できますか？

◆ **Pre-Reading Question**

How can we control ourselves so that we don't get stuck on the hedonic treadmill?

◆ **Vocabulary**

1. Benefits 利点
2. Depressed 落ちこむ
3. Effort 努力
4. Predicting 予測

◆ **Fill in each blank in the sentences below with the correct word.**

a. Yumi put a lot of _____ into the paper and got an A+ for her work.

b. The article discussed the many health _____ of avoiding sugar.

c. Many sports writers are _____ that David will be the most valuable basketball player.

d. "Sometimes I get so_____ listening to news right now, I feel like crying," my friend said.

◆ Reading 🎧 ¹³

*"I make myself rich by making my wants few." – **Henry David Thoreau***

[1] To prevent ourselves from becoming stuck on the hedonic treadmill, we must understand the effect that the desire to own and possess things has on us. Today, it is very easy to constantly update our "stuff." Products of all kinds are advertised as being "new and improved" to try to get us to buy more. And, of course, we do, in an effort to increase our status and happiness. But the thing is, these feelings and benefits do not last long – perhaps three to six months, if we're lucky!

[2] Some people crave a life of luxury. They believe that with greater income and greater success, and by buying and possessing ever-more expensive things, they will be happier and more admired. They feel that owning luxury goods expresses who they are. But we humans are poor at predicting how long this happiness lasts. Yes, we become happier when we reach a certain level of life security – when we have the basics: decent food, adequate clothing, a decent place to live. But there is no evidence that our happiness increases as we pile up possessions. In fact, it appears that the opposite is true. By putting so much effort into maintaining the hedonic treadmill, we unfortunately waste huge amounts of time and energy (not to mention money) in order to organize and protect everything. Over time, our stress levels can increase to the point where we harm our health and may become seriously depressed.

[3] How can we get off the hedonic treadmill? Think of all the things you like to do – all the activities you enjoy. A key to happiness is to alternate these activities. Don't get stuck doing one thing for so long that the thrill of doing it wears off. Remember, if you become bored with one activity, you can change it and do something else for a while. For a big happiness boost, surprise yourself and do something completely different. Let's say you have five pastimes that you really love. Don't do just one of them nonstop every day for days on end. Do one on Monday, another on Tuesday, and so on. That way, you'll never become bored with any of them. They will all retain their pleasure and excitement.

[4] Cherishing our memories is another way to get off the hedonic treadmill, just as having experiences that create new memories also offer a lifetime of benefits. Unlike material goods, our memories and life experiences get better with time. Why? Because there are few greater

pleasures than recalling and talking about our experiences – even the not so good ones. Many of the things we do are nice, even amazing as we experience them. But their real value is in the future when they take on new life in our memory – when we can talk about them, relive them, and share them with others.

[5] All of us are on our own hedonic treadmill. The first step in not letting our treadmill get out of control is to be grateful for what we have. Learn to enjoy the small pleasures life offers us. But also, always keep in mind that pleasures are brief, especially those related to buying and owning "stuff." So know when you have enough. Train yourself to be happier with less.

"A house is just a place to keep your stuff while you go out and get more stuff."
– George Carlin

◆ Active Outline

1. These days, it is _____ to update the things that you own. **(easy / difficult)**

2. Those who wish to live a life of luxury often purchase _____ items.
   (older / more expensive / cheaper)

   a. People are _____ at predicting how long their happiness will last after they get some nice or expensive thing. **(good / poor)**

   b. If we put too much effort into maintaining the hedonic treadmill, the experience is overall a _____ one. **(positive / negative)**

3. To increase your happiness, one idea is to do _____ things every once in a while.
   (the same / different)

4. It is our _____ that actually get better with time. **(possessions / memories)**

5. To get off the hedonic treadmill, you should try to be happier with _____ goods.
   (more / fewer)

◆ Comprehension

1. To get off the treadmill, we must give up purchasing new things altogether. **(True / False)**

2. You should alternate your hobbies and interests so that you don't get tired of them.
   (True / False)

3. When we wish to buy something nice, what happens? Put the following steps in the order in which they occur.

    A . We no longer use or enjoy the thing and set it aside.

    B . We get used to and even tired of our new thing.

    C . We see or think about a thing we want.

    D . We go out and buy that thing.

    E . We go out and buy another thing.

    F . We initially feel a boost of happiness.

    1. ____   2. ____   3. ____   4. ____   5. ____   6. ____

◆ Critical / Creative Thinking

List three of the nicest, most expensive items that you own and then list three of your most positive experiences or memories.

Your nicest items	Your most positive experiences / memories
1. _____	1. _____
2. _____	2. _____
3. _____	3. _____

◆ Discussion

Discuss these in groups. What was your level of happiness you felt on a scale of 1 to 10, ten being the highest, while discussing each?

While rating the items, I felt a happiness level of _____. This was because _____

_____.

While rating the experiences, I felt a happiness level of _____. This was because _____

_____.

Opinion

Based upon my ratings, I can see that it is (items / experiences) that make me happier. This is because _____

_____.

◆ Word Fill

Fill in the blanks with either "experiences" or "material goods."

Traditionally, people have thought that it is better to purchase **(1)** _____. The reason for this is that such things can be seen, touched, and admired by others. They have real value and may even eventually be sold for a profit. On the other hand, **(2)** _____ disappear almost as soon as we have them. Even so, in terms of happiness, it is better to have **(3)** _____ since talking about your **(4)** _____ after the event actually increases or, at least, helps you relive the joy you felt at the time. People who talk about their **(5)** _____ are often considered self-centered and insecure – or, sometimes, just boring. The problem is when we talk about our "stuff," we start to compare our **(6)** _____ – how much they cost, how famous they are, and on and on. But because no two people can ever have the same **(7)** _____, **(8)** _____ cannot be compared in the same way. There's really no comparison, say, between enjoying a wonderful concert and the joy of learning a new skill. What is perhaps most interesting about **(9)** _____ and **(10)** _____ is that as time goes by, with the former our level of happiness keeps on increasing, while with the latter as time goes by our happiness levels decreases.

◆ Comprehension

Circle the correct words to complete the quote.

"Part of us believe the new car is better because it **1. (lasts / does not last)** longer. But in fact that's the **2. (best / worst)** thing about the new car …. A new car sticks around to disappoint you. But a trip to Europe **3. (continues / is soon over)**. It evaporates. It has the good sense to go away, and you are left with nothing but a **4. (wonderful / terrible)** memory." *–Daniel Gilbert*

> **Opinion: Do you agree with this quote? Why or why not?**

I (**agree / do not agree**) with this quote because _____

_____.

For example _____

_____.

◆ Discussion / Writing

Write brief answers to these questions and then discuss them.

I. How much effort do you put into the hedonic treadmill? Explain.

_____

_____

_____

II. Whom do you know who spends too much time and effort on the treadmill? What happens?

_____

_____

_____

III. What one word describes the way that you shop? Do you have a "shopping problem"? Explain.

_____

_____

_____

Make up some questions of your own that are related to today's reading. *Be creative!!*

The Relationship between Cats and People

猫と人の関係

◆ Pre-Reading Question

How and when did cats become humans' pets and begin to share our lives?

◆ Vocabulary:

1. Companionship 友交（関係）
2. Gorgeous 素敵
3. Handled 処理
4. Kitty litter 猫用トイレ
5. Loneliness 孤独

◆ **Match the sentence beginnings with their endings.**

1. Without the **kitty litter**, _____ a. was made by hand.

2. **Handle** the vase with care _____ b. the house would smell really bad.

3. If you want **companionship**, _____ c. why not join a social club?

4. Tom felt deep **loneliness** _____ d. because it is very fragile.

5. This **gorgeous** furniture _____ e. after his long-time partner left.

"As every cat owner knows, nobody owns a cat." – **Ellen Perry Berkeley**

[1] The relationship between humans and cats may have begun around ten thousand years ago. Back then, people living in villages would store their crops; however, the problem was that rats and mice would sneak in and eat the stored corn or wheat. But cats would then eat these pests, and the villagers' problem was solved. Catching on to how useful cats could be to them, slowly but surely, villagers decided to keep them as around as pets. They kept cats with them even as they moved from place to place around the world. It was a perfect relationship that has lasted many, many thousands of years.

[2] But quite recently, something happened that completely changed our relationship with cats. Until then, most cats had been kept outdoors. They weren't the household pets that we know and love today. But in 1947, "Kitty Litter" was created, completely by accident. This incredible new product had a huge impact: It stopped the strong smells and messes that cats made and that had kept them outside. This huge change opened the door for cats to move inside their owners' homes, where they have lived quite happily and comfortably ever since.

[3] There are a few things to keep in mind about how cats are able to enjoy a relationship with people. For this to happen, it should be handled – stroked and petted – before it is eight weeks old. Otherwise, the cat may resist and keep itself distant from us. The more a young cat is handled, the friendlier it becomes. Obviously, then, a cat that is petted an hour a day will be closer to humans than one that is handled just 15 minutes a day. Ideally, to make the young cat more accepting, people of all kinds – young and old, male and female – should "cuddle" it as often as possible.

[4] Playing and just being with a cat provides us humans with all kinds of benefits. For one thing, spending just a little time with a cat provides us with companionship and relaxation. It boosts our mental and emotional health by lowering stress levels, reducing loneliness, and even preventing depression. Research has shown that the time we spend with our cats has physical benefits, too. It helps lower blood pressure and can prevent heart disease, thereby improving our overall health and well-being.

[5] What is it about cats that makes them such beloved companions? Perhaps it is their independence; most cats don't need to be constantly pleased as dogs do. Although cats do like to be handled and get attention, it doesn't take as much to satisfy them. Just give them a bit of food and water, and they can pretty much take care of themselves – and they sleep a lot, so they are really no bother at all. They also help get rid of household pests such as mice, rats, and even some bugs. And one additional benefit is that cats have a sort of mysterious air about them that we humans are very attracted to.

[6] Cats are the most popular pet in the world today. By 1985, for the first time ever, more Americans had pet cats than pet dogs, with an equal number of men and women being cat owners. Cat owners by and large really love their cats and feel that theirs are absolutely gorgeous. Perhaps it's because their small round faces, tiny noses, and big round eyes resemble the cutest human baby. Some people argue that cats are cold and too independent, but the fact is that cats can and do become just as attached to people as dogs. Cats have a long memory and many do become extremely close to their human companions.

"The love for all living creatures is the most noble attribute of man." – ***Charles Darwin***

◆ Active Outline

1. People and cats first began their relationship around _____.
   (ten thousand years ago / hundreds of years ago / twenty years ago / 1947)

   a. Cats were helpful in controlling _____. **(mice and rats / crops / food)**

2. Since 1947, kitty litter has allowed cats to _____.
   (live inside / live outside / be handled)

3. The more a young cat is handled, the more _____ it becomes.
   (distant / friendly / difficult)

4. Cats are known to help people _____.
   (relax / boost their moods / lower their stress levels / all of these)

5. Perhaps humans like cats so much because they are so _____.
   (independent / dependent / demanding)

6. The most popular pet in the world today is the _____. **(dog / cat)**

   a. The number of male cat owners in America is _____ the number of female cat owners.
      (larger than / smaller than / the same as)

◆ Word Scramble

Unscramble the words to make complete sentences.

1. only people's / Cats / their health. / moods, but also / improve not

_____

2. more cats / America. / dogs in / there were / In 1985, / than

_____

3. to / people become / their cats? / Why do / so close

_____

4. friendlier to you / How do you / and your family? / train your pet / to become

_____

5. popular. / Cats had / around the / them even more / spread all / world, making

_____

6. never have moved / cats / people's homes. / into / would / Without kitty litter

_____

◆ Sentence Matching

Match the unscrambled sentences above with the paragraphs in today's reading in which the sentence's information can be found.

Paragraph 1. Sentence: _____   Paragraph 2. Sentence: _____

Paragraph 3. Sentence: _____   Paragraph 4. Sentence: _____

Paragraph 5. Sentence: _____   Paragraph 6. Sentence: _____

◆ Critical / Creative Thinking

Give four reasons – some from the text, some of your own, why people love their cats.

1. _____   2. _____

3. _____   4. _____

◆ Agree or Disagree

Read these statements and circle "agree" or "disagree." Explain your reasons.

1. I like cats more than dogs.

   I (agree / disagree) with this because _____

   _____.

2. Pets can improve people's health.

   I (agree / disagree) with this because _____

   _____.

3. Pets can understand words or emotions.

   I (agree / disagree) with this because _____

   _____.

4. I am planning to own a pet in the future.

   I (agree / disagree) with this because _____

   _____.

5. There are differences between people who prefer cats and people who prefer dogs.

   I (agree / disagree) with this because _____

   _____.

6. Make up and write your own "Agree or Disagree?" sentence here.

   _____.

   I (agree / disagree) with this because _____

   _____.

◆ Discussion / Writing

Write brief answers to the questions below. Then share your ideas with a partner.

I. Some studies have concluded that people with pets live longer. Do you think this is true? Explain.

_____

_____

_____

II. Can people really love their pets? Can cats (or pets in general) really love their owners? Explain.

_____

_____

_____

III. Can a pet be like a member of the family? Why or why not?

_____

_____

_____

IV. If you were stuck on a desert island, would you prefer to have your favorite pet(s) with you or to have your husband, wife, boyfriend, girlfriend or best friend with you? Why?

_____

_____

_____

Make up some questions of your own that are related to today's reading. Be creative!!

14

The Power of Forgiveness, Part 1:
Why Forgive?

許しの力 Part 1：なぜ許すのか

◆ **Pre-Reading Question**

Is there someone you need to forgive? How important is it for you to do so?

◆ **Vocabulary**

1. Apologize 謝罪   2. Peacefully 平和的に   3. Relationships 関係
4. Revenge 復讐   5. Wounds 傷

◆ Match the words with their meanings or descriptions.

a. _____   Calmly; free from stress

b. _____   How people are connected

c. _____   Emotional pain, suffering, and injuries

d. _____   To say you are sorry

e. _____   To try to hurt someone who has hurt you; get back at

◆ Reading 🎧 15

"Forgive others. Not because they deserve forgiveness, but because you deserve peace."
– Jonathan Lockwood Huire

[1] Someone has done something to you that has hurt or offended you deeply. Should you forgive that person? Psychological research shows that the answer to that question is a definite yes. But maybe not for the reasons you might think. The fact is, if we do not forgive those people, that we very often pay the price in growing inner pain or increased stress. But once we do manage to forgive another person, we gain not only peace of mind, but we also gain all kinds of other benefits: better physical and mental health; an improved sense of self-worth; and healthier, stronger relationships. But unfortunately, many of us can't do it. We hold on to our old wounds and they only get worse throughout our lifetimes – and we pay the price for it in deep unhappiness and dissatisfaction with life.

[2] So the question becomes: How can we find the will to forgive and let go? The first step in the process – and it's not an easy one, of course – is to not wait for the other person to apologize. Begin the process within yourself. Yes, you have a dark, heavy feeling inside you. You do recall what happened, and often relive those painful moments. It hurts, really hurts. But holding all that anger and resentment inside you only makes the hurt worse. And maybe even worse, it's a waste of time. The longer you wait to forgive, the longer you will suffer stress, which can result in low energy, sleepless nights, and perhaps even serious health problems. So don't put forgiving off. And remember – and this is a key point – forgiveness is about making you yourself feel better. It's about easing your own suffering and giving you peace.

[3] We may wish for revenge – to somehow get back at and hurt the person who has hurt us. We think, I have been wronged, and for no reason. I haven't done anything "bad." So why do I have to be the one who forgives? But the fact is, to seek revenge is not a healthy or effective way to deal with our negative emotions. Consider that perhaps the other person is probably feeling a lot of pain as well. And if I'm honest, maybe there's more to the problem than I've realized. Then ask yourself: How can I move on and create a more peaceful and happier me?

[4] This may make forgiving and forgetting sound easy, and, to be sure it isn't. Forgiving

another takes time. But without forgiveness, without apologizing, you can never free yourself from the past. You will never be able to truly move forward. Keeping those negative feelings locked up inside you is like a wound that stays wide open; it even eats at the soul. When you have the courage to forgive, the other person does not have control over that wound, so that you can finally heal. You feel lighter, freer, stronger, happier. You regain control over your feelings and recover your personal energy. You can then, and only then, get back on the path to a more peaceful, productive, and joyful life.

"To forgive is to set a prisoner free and discover that the prisoner was you."
– Lewis B. Smedes

◆ Active Outline

1. If you do not forgive another person, it is often _____ who suffers the most.

   (you / the other person)

   a. When you forgive another person, you experience improved _____ health.

      (physical / mental / both of these / neither of these)

2. You should wait for the other person to apologize before you begin the process of healing.
   (True / False)

3. You should in some way get back at, or take revenge upon, any person who has hurt you.
   (True / False)

4. To "forgive and forget" is much easier said than done. **(True / False)**

◆ Word Scramble

Unscramble the words to make complete sentences.

1. is a waste / cause / Holding on / and can / to your anger / health problems. / of time

   _____

2. live / so you can / to get rid of your / negative feelings / a stress-free life. / It is important

   _____

3. no one is perfect. / To forgive / person, you / the other / and know that / that person well / can wish

   _____

4. take the time / Do not / person, but / that person / the other / to forgive / try to hurt / and move on.

   _____

5. for a lifetime. / It is important / hold on / others; / to our hurt feelings / to forgive / otherwise, we can

   _____

◆ Sentence Matching

Match the unscrambled sentences above with the paragraphs in today's reading in which the sentence's information can be found. Note that one sentence is not used.

Paragraph 1. Sentence: _____   Paragraph 2. Sentence: _____

Paragraph 3. Sentence: _____   Paragraph 4. Sentence: _____

◆ Dialogue Build

Below is a conversation between a person who was bullied and a friend of that person. What does each person say and in what order? Write the lines in the proper place in the chart below.

- Perhaps one day I will.

- Back then, I was overweight and wore big old clothes to try to hide it. All the other children made fun of me.

- Well, today my life is filled with good friends, and I love my school.

- I found out that the parents of the person who made up that name were getting a divorce.

- They called me "Frog" because I was so heavy and fat and had a big chin.

- I hope that you will eventually stop feeling so angry and forgive the person.

- Oh, really. What happened?

- What a horrible thing to say.

Person Bullied	Her Friend
As a child, perhaps no one was bullied more than I was.	1.
2.	What did they do?
3.	It was really mean of them to make fun of your body and face.
Yes. They would shout out that name while we were on the bus every day.	4.

5.	We all handle things like that in different ways. It looks as if the person handled it with anger towards you.
6.	It is great that today, things are going so well for you.
Yes. Everything is far better than I could have imagined compared to those days when I used to ride the bus.	7.
8.	

◆ Complete the Sentences

Write a sentence beginning for each sentence ending below. Use information from today's reading.

1. _____ to have better physical and mental health.

2. _____ can never forget those terrible memories.

3. _____ not a healthy way to deal with your emotions.

4. _____ sounds easy, it is actually quite difficult to do.

5. _____ so that you can have peace in your life.

6. Make up your own ending of a sentence about today's topic.

_____.

7. Now write the beginning of your sentence.

_____.

◆ Discussion / Writing

I. Do you think that forgiving others is as important as today's reading claims? Why or why not? Give an example.

I (**think / don't think**) that forgiving others is so important. This is because _____

_____

_____ .

For example, _____

_____ .

II. Is it difficult for you to forgive another person? Why or why not?

For me, it (**is / is not**) difficult to forgive someone else. This is because _____

_____

_____ .

III. How can we forgive another person?

One way to forgive another person is by _____

_____

_____ .

Make up some questions of your own that are related to today's reading. Be creative!!

15

The Power of Forgiveness, Part II:
How to Forgive
許しの力 Part 2：許す方法

◆ **Pre-Reading Question**

How can you forgive another person?

◆ **Vocabulary**

> 1. Harm 危害
> 2. Journey 旅
> 3. Pain 痛み
> 4. Self-compassion 自己憐憫

◆ **Fill in the blanks in each description with the correct word.**

a. The word _____ means "damage" as in "Pollution is causing the environment great _____" or "When moving, be careful not to _____ the furniture."

b. The word _____ is a synonym for "ache" or "suffering," and can be used for a physical or emotional hurt.

c. The word _____ refers to the act of traveling from one place to another. Perhaps it is a real trip, or a life passage of some sort, as in "This story is about my _____ from youth to maturity."

d. The word _____ is best defined as "our ability to feel the same sense of understanding and forgiveness for ourselves as we feel for others."

◆ Reading 🎧 16

*"Holding on to anger is like grasping a hot coal with the intent of throwing it at someone else; you are the one who gets burned." – **Buddha***

[1] Forgiving another person can be as quick and easy as saying, "I forgive you." But for those who have really hurt you, actually forgiving someone can take years. You don't ever forget what happened, nor do you really excuse it. What you are doing is simply accepting the fact that no one is perfect – that we all make mistakes and cause one another harm or pain from time to time. In this sense, forgiveness becomes the act of changing your negative feelings into positive ones. How do you do this? There are many ways to begin your journey toward forgiveness – and to personal growth.

[2] To help you get rid of your negative feelings, write them down in a journal. Explain in detail how you were harmed and why what happened upset or hurt you so deeply. Be honest with yourself. Put down everything you want to say. Don't let anything be left unsaid!

[3] Another technique to change your negative feelings into more positive ones is to write a letter that forgives the person for all the harm that he or she has caused you. In the letter, you might say something like, "I forgive you for lying to me" or "What you did to me made me feel terrible, but I forgive you." Whether what you write is completely true or not do not really matter. What matters is that you release your negativity and try to truly feel the forgiveness.

[4] Look at what happened as a learning experience. No matter what has been said or done to you, be thankful for what the other person has taught you. Remind yourself that you have something to learn from everyone and every experience, even the negative ones. Perhaps the experience helped you grow not only in being able to feel compassion for others, but also in feeling self-compassion. Perhaps what happened helped you understand yourself better and actually made you stronger.

[5] Try to put yourself in the other person's position. Ask yourself: What made this person behave this way? What has life done to make him so angry? Why would she want to cause you harm? If you can better understand the other person's motives, it may increase your ability to feel compassion, which can lead to better understanding all around. This does not mean that what the person did was acceptable or right. But knowing why the person did it helps you to understand that no one is perfect, which is a big step.

[6] Feel the pain you have inside you. Ask yourself where in your body you feel it. Actually point to it. Feel that space within your body. Then, after you have located the pain, give it a name. This may sound like an odd thing to do, but naming your negative feelings is a simple but powerful technique to make that emotion easier to manage.

[7] Tell someone else about the pain you are feeling. Find a trusted friend or professional and tell them what happened and how you feel about it, and then listen to what they have to say about it.

[8] Sincerely, genuinely wish the person who harmed you the best in life. Imagine him or her being happy or successful. If you can do this, you have made real progress. This is a tough but essential step in your journey to real forgiveness. You might take this step a bit further by secretly sending the person a little gift or even some money to help out in some way. When you can honestly wish the best for that person, you have reached a new level of wealth in a truly meaningful sense.

[9] Being hurt is a human feeling that we all share. Knowing that you are not alone can help ease your anger and pain. Also, be gentle with yourself, and know that you deserve to be happy. After all, when you forgive another, you are not only helping that person: You are helping yourself.

"Always forgive your enemies – nothing annoys them so much."
– Oscar Wilde

◆ Active Outline

Read the statements below and decide if they are true or false.

1. Forgiving someone who has hurt you can take years. **True / False**

2. One way to forgive someone is to write down your feelings about that person. **True / False**

3. When you write your feelings in a letter of forgiveness, everything you write must be absolutely true. **True / False**

4. You can learn from everyone, even people who have hurt you. **True / False**

5. Putting yourself in another person's place is not an effective way to better understand that person. **True / False**

6. When you locate the pain you feel inside your body, you should give it a name, so as to make it easier to manage. **True / False**

7. You should never speak of these with a friend or professional. **True / False**

8. Wishing the person who harmed you well is impossible, so you shouldn't even try. **True / False**

9. When you forgive another person, at the same time you are also helping yourself. **True / False**

◆ Matching

Match each sentence with the correct paragraph number from today's reading.

_____ Wish that person the best.

_____ Learn, even from those who have hurt you.

__2__ Write your feelings down in a diary.

_____ Imagine being the other person so as, to better understand their point of view.

_____ Know that you are not alone, and that many other people feel just as you do.

_____ Change your negative feelings to positive ones.

_____ Find and feel the hurt inside yourself, and give it a name.

_____ Write a letter of forgiveness to the person who has harmed you.

_____ Tell a friend or professional about what happened and how it made you feel.

◆ Fill in the Blanks

Select two of the sentences above and explain why you "would" or "would not" be able to follow the advice about how to forgive someone. Complete your explanation by then filling in the blanks.

Example Do you think that you can _2_? Would it be helpful? Why or why not?

I think that _writing down my feelings in a diary_ (would / **would not**) be helpful.

This is because _I am not good at expressing my feelings by writing them down_.

1. Do you think that you can _____? Would it be helpful? Why or why not?

I think that _____ (would / would not) be helpful. This is because

_____

_____.

2. Do you think that you can _____? Would it be helpful? Why or why not?

I think that _____ (would / would not) be helpful. This is because

_____

_____.

◆ Reverse Questions

Write the questions that you would need to ask to get the answers below.

1. **Question:** *Is it* _____? *How* _____?

   Answer: No, actually to forgive someone can be a difficult process that can take years.

2. **Question:** *What is one way* _____
   _____?

   Answer: You can write such feelings down in a journal.

3. **Question:** *Do you think life* _____
   _____?

   Answer: Yes. I believe that the person probably had a difficult time while growing up.

4. **Question:** *Am I* _____
   _____?

   Answer: No, you are not alone. Everyone has similar emotions.

5. **Question:** *Where in your body can you* _____
   _____?

   Answer: I can feel the pain in my stomach.

6. **Question:** *Should I* _____
   _____?

   Answer: By all means! If you can wish the person well, you have made incredible progress.

◆ Discussion / Writing

I. Of the methods for forgiving another person that are listed in today's reading, which one do you think is the best? Why do you like or prefer it?

_____

_____

_____

II. What other ways can you think of that we can use to help forgive another person?

_____

_____

_____

Make up some questions of your own that are related to today's reading. *Be creative!!*

Life Topics: Changing Views　　　　　　　　　　　　　　　　　[B-949]
総合英語　ライフトピックス 5

1　　刷　　2023年 3月 7日

著　者　　ジョナサン・バーマン　　Jonathan Berman

発行者　　南雲　一範　Kazunori Nagumo
発行所　　株式会社　南雲堂
　　　　　〒162-0801　東京都新宿区山吹町361
　　　　　NAN'UN-DO Co., Ltd.
　　　　　361 Yamabuki-cho, Shinjuku-ku, Tokyo 162-0801, Japan
　　　　　振替口座：00160-0-46863
　　　　　TEL: 03-3268-2311（営業部：学校関係）
　　　　　　　　03-3268-2384（営業部：書店関係）
　　　　　　　　03-3268-2387（編集部）
　　　　　FAX: 03-3269-2486

編集者　　加藤　敦

製　版　　中西　史子

装　丁　　銀月堂

検　印　　省　略

コード　　ISBN978-4-523-17949-8　　C0082

Printed in Japan

E-mail　nanundo@post.email.ne.jp
URL　https://www.nanun-do.co.jp/